What people ar
Van Me...

MW00462409

"Some of the most significant cryptozoological research is occurring on little-known historical cases, such as the one captured in this intriguing volume. Winged weirdies like the Van Meter Visitor are not to be taken lightly, and I, for one, am appreciative that an in-depth examination by these outstanding investigators has been undertaken."

—**Loren Coleman,** Director, International Cryptozoology Museum, Portland, Maine, and author of over 30 books.

~

"The Van Meter Visitor came and left in the dark in 1903...OR DID IT?"

—**Jolena Welker,** Van Meter Public Library Director

~

"Iowa—it's not just for cornfields anymore. Did a flock of horned, bat-winged monsters visit the small town of Van Meter, Iowa in 1903? This little-known but horrific episode in American history is laid out and dissected in chilling detail by the adventurous, investigative trio of Noah Voss, Chad Lewis, and Kevin Nelson. Highly recommended for fans of cryptozoology, horror, and the paranormal alike!"

—**Linda S. Godfrey**, author of *Real Wolfmen: True Encounters in Modern America* and numerous other award-winning books. Find her books, blog and other info at lindagodfrey.com.

THE
VAN METER
VISITOR

A TRUE AND MYSTERIOUS ENCOUNTER
WITH THE UNKNOWN

THE

VAN METER

VISITOR

A TRUE AND MYSTERIOUS ENCOUNTER WITH THE UNKNOWN

BY
CHAD LEWIS
NOAH VOSS
KEVIN LEE NELSON

ON THE ROAD PUBLICATIONS

The Van Meter Visitor:
A True & Mysterious Encounter with the Unknown

by
Chad Lewis, Noah Voss, and Kevin Nelson
Foreword by Brad Steiger

ISBN: 978-0982431467

Proudly printed in the United States by Documation

On The Road Publications
3204 Venus Ave
Eau Claire, WI 54703
www.chadlewisresearch.com

Cover Design: Kevin Lee Nelson

DEDICATION

This book is dedicated to the people of 1903 Van Meter who not only lived through the encounter, they preserved it for the rest of us to enjoy.

TABLE OF CONTENTS

FOREWORD
BY BRAD STEIGER

In 1974, after the success of my book *Mysteries of Time and Space: The Riddle of Impossible Fossils, Unsettling Relics, Photographic Anomalies and How to Explain Them*, I was astonished at the trust and generosity of readers who sent me their own "unsettling relics" that they had in their possession—everything from strange coins, fossilized footprints, to old photos of strange, cryptid beings. Among these items sent for my examination was a 48-page booklet bound in leather entitled *The Piasa or The Devil Among the Indians* (Morris, Illinois, 1887) by P.A. Armstrong. This remarkable text told of a huge birdlike creature that preyed upon the tribes that lived near what is today Alton, Illinois. According to the account, the monster "had the wings of bat, but in the shape of an eagle's...four legs supplied with eagle like talons...the body of a dragon or alligator...the face of a man...the horns of a black-tailed deer or elk...the teeth of a tiger...the tail of a serpent...the scales of a salamander."

As an Iowa farm lad, I had a habit of frequently diverting my attention from the rows of crops that I was cultivating to glance upward, hoping to see a hawk, an eagle, or some other great winged bird. Actually, I was hoping to see some surviving pterodactyl soaring above me. But I would not have welcomed the sight of the Piasa overhead selecting me for a snack in the same manner that it dined on the Native Americans of the Mississippi near Alton.

When my friend Noah Voss told me that he was writing an examination of the famous Van Meter, Iowa, "Visitor," with his colleagues Chad Lewis and Kevin Nelson, he immediately aroused my interest. The strange visitation by an eight-foot, bat-winged, horned humanoid took place in 1903, and it remains a classic case of high strangeness. At the time of the alleged visitation, the monster spread panic and hysteria to the people of the community, whose theories ranged from a demonic creature of darkness to the Prince of Darkness himself. I was immediately curious just how the three researchers would deal with the creature and the additional mystery of whether it was itself glowing or whether it somehow bore a bright light with it on its late night visitations.

In the native tongue "Iowa/Ioway" means "this is the place." And the state has certainly been the "place" for numerous reports of haunting, UFO sightings, strange creature sightings. And when it comes to reports of gigantic winged beings, consider this small sampling:

The Bedford Times-Independent, Bedford, Iowa, August 11, 1887, reported that a man named Lee Corder encountered a flying serpent "…writhing and twisting, with protruding eyes and forked tongue. Great scales, which glistened in the sunlight, covered its huge body, which appeared to be flat and nearly a foot in width."

The newspaper described Mr. Corder as a man of "unimpeachable veracity," and goes on to state that he, and those with him, watched the flying serpent with "awe and astonishment," as the creature landed in a cornfield, a few rods distant with a dull thud. The witnesses who observed the creature, all professed to be so frightened that none of them wished to block its path, and it was permitted to pass on its way "unmolested" to return to the sky.

******

In October, 1890, citizens of Independence, Iowa, reported seeing a monster with "wings, a monstrous head with horns, a mouth like an alligator's. Its body was greenish in color and covered with shiny scales; its eyes glare like an electric arc light; and it yells in a tone that sounds like a combination of the roar of a lion and the scream of a wildcat."

******

Tim lives in western Clinton county, Iowa, about a mile from the Wapsipinicon River. Back in 1986, he was out hunting squirrels when he sighted a really big bird. It stood over six-feet tall on the branch where it wasperching. It was very bronze and black in color. In some ways it resembled a very large eagle.

One evening a few nights later, Tim was attending a camp ground event on "Birds of Prey in the Midwest."

"I described the giant bird in detail for the biologist," Tim said, "but the scientist told me that such a bird was impossible. There were no birds in the Americas larger than a condor, and there were no condors in Iowa."

(Personal correspondence May 28, 2004.)

******

Returning to the nearby state of Illinois, where the Piasa feasted on tribes people in its cave overlooking the Mississippi, according to the November 20, 1930 issue of the Cairo, Illinois, *Democrat,* James Henry of Mound City shot an unknown bird on the Kentucky shore, opposite that city, which was described as being larger than an ostrich, and weighed one hundred and four pounds. The newspaper went on to describe "… its head is of a fiery red. The wings, of deep black, measured fifteen feet from tip to tip, and the bill, of a yellow color, twenty-four inches. Its legs are slender and sinewy, pea green in color, and measure forty-eight inches in length. One of the feet resemble that of a duck, and the other that of a turkey.

"Henry shot it at a distance of one hundred yards, from the top-most branch of a dead tree, where it had perched preying upon a full-sized sheep that it had carried from the ground."

Experts speculated that the "strange species of bird," no doubt had "existed extensively during the days of the mastodon, is almost entirely extinct— the last one having been seen in the state of New York during the year 1812." The giant bird with the fifteen-foot wing span was exhibited in an office in Mound City and drew hundreds of curious citizens, who had witnessed the creature on its flight across the town and river. (Thanks to Jerome Clark for the newspaper clipping quoted above.)

******

On April 9, 1948, a farm family outside of Caledonia, Illinois, saw a monster bird that they described as larger than an airplane. A Freeport truck driver said that he, too, had seen the creature on the same day. A former army colonel admitted that he had seen it while he stood talking with the head of Western Military Academy and a farmer near Alton. "It was a bird of tremendous size," he said.

On April 10, several witnesses saw the gigantic bird in the skies over Illinois. "I thought it was a type of plane that I had never seen before," one percipient said. "It was circling and banking in a way I had never seen a plane perform. I kept waiting for it to fall."

On April 24, back at Alton [the legendary home of the Piasa], a man described what he saw as an enormous, incredible thing flying at about five hundred feet.

******

In addition to having written a fascinating book, the authors must be commended for approaching the mystery from a number of different aspects.

Did the initial sighting of some strange creature or phenomenon bring about a kind of mass hysteria in the community and the surrounding environs?

Was the Visitor a hitherto unknown cyrptid, a kind of Bigfoot with batlike wings?

Could the appearance of the winged monster have been a distraction for UFO activity? Perhaps even an abduction of one or more of Van Meter's inhabitants?

Was the manifestation of the Visitor an example of an ultra terrestrial entity, who was quite literally a "visitor" from another dimension of reality?

Or was the entire incident an elaborate hoax in order to create the kind of publicity that brings the curious to see for themselves if they might catch a glimpse of the hideous Van Meter Visitor?

I guarantee that you will find the research, the theories, and the fascination that Noah Voss, Chad Lewis, and Kevin Nelson bring to their examination of this provocative mystery to hold your interest with the steady grip of the skilled writers that they are.

—Brad Steiger

ACKNOWLEDGEMENTS

First and foremost we want to thank Jolena Welker because without her research and assistance this book would not be what it is today. The same goes for Vickie Benson and the rest of the people at the Van Meter Public Library.

Along the way many of our friends and family played a huge role in this project and we want to thank them all especially Ryel Estes for her loving support and solid advice; Gary & Adonna Nelson for their continuous encouragement; Nisa Giaquinto and Leo Lewis for always being the most unique creatures out there; and Jennifer Voss for her enduring stoicism of dark and dangerous adventures.

Thank you Sarah Szymanski for once again working your magic on this text.

To our fellow researchers: Todd "Summerwind" Roll, Linda Godfrey, Dennis Boyer for reminding us that the land holds many secrets, and Richard Hendricks—researcher extraordinaire.

Special thanks to: The Headhunter's Hideaway for always staying open late for us, *Wisconsin Today*, and to all the small-town bars and diners that provided us with great food, beers, and countless leads.

Those researchers who came before us, breaking the ground on the areas of study such as ultraterrestrials that remain too edgy for most even in the fringe field of paranormal investigation especially John Keel, Jacques Vallee, Brad Steiger, and Charles Fort.

WHERE IS VAN METER?

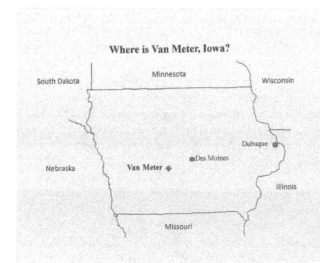

HISTORY

1
Unearthing a Legend
by Chad Lewis

With just days left before we embarked on our legend trip through Iowa, I simply couldn't shake the nagging uneasiness that some integral part of the trip was missing. Even though Noah Voss, Kevin Nelson and I planned to investigate some of Iowa's most unusual places, the trip seemed to lack a real backbone. Usually the last few days before a big investigation were filled with bubbling anticipation and excitement, which is why I was baffled as to why I felt such ambivalence regarding this upcoming legend trip. As someone who thoroughly enjoys spending an inordinate amount of time on the road researching folklore and lecturing on the findings, my sudden ho-hum attitude on travel was quite perplexing. It wasn't as though the proposed trip lacked of excitement or adventure. On the contrary, the itinerary that we had mapped out included the investigation of a cursed angel statue that brought death to those who visited it, a secluded bridge where a large werewolf creature prowled, and a half dozen other haunted locations that were flush with tales of ghosts and spirits. Perhaps my unwelcome dreariness resided in the fact that, over the years, at least one of us had already been to the majority of the places on our destination…the curse of any seasoned legend tripper.

Many years ago I began the tedious task of scouring through old newspapers for the first book in my "Hidden Headlines" series, *Hidden Headlines of Wisconsin*. The book featured several hundred Wisconsin newspaper articles from 1860-1910 that described cases of bizarre deaths, peculiar people, psychic phenomena, UFOs, ghosts, and an assortment of other extraordinarily strange cases. Several years ago, after completing a few other "Hidden Headlines" books on various states, I began digging up strange Iowa-based articles. The project kept getting sidelined by other, more pressing book deadlines, and so the nearly forgotten research was relegated to a folder in the back of my file cabinet. With my anxiety about the impending Iowa legend trip growing, I decided to rummage through the old cases hoping that something bizarre and intriguing would pop out. Time had placed some distance between me and these stories. I had slowly forgotten how truly odd these cases were—as I flipped through the articles, each one became weirder than the next. Tales of a woman being frightened to death gave way to a vengeful male spirit haunting his alleged killer. As I slowly made my way though the huge stack of one-hundred-year-old articles I often paused to re-read stories about a man driven crazy by religion, or the mysterious airship that was buzzing over Iowa towns. After a few hours of reading these tantalizing articles, I began to lose faith in the possibility of finding that one special case that could anchor the legend trip… that is until I ran across the article titled "Des Moines' New Monster." The 1903 article claimed that "two weird-looking terror-striking monsters are living in an abandoned coal mine on the edge of town." I was immediately hooked by the sheer oddness contained in the story. Amazingly, a quick check of the research showed that, outside of a few cursory mentions of the case, no real investigation of any kind had been conducted into the mysterious events of 1903.

The overall lack of national familiarity with some older cases isn't that uncommon. Over the years, I have discovered that what at first seems like an unknown legend is only unknown for those who don't reside in the immediate area where the legend originated. While most paranormal legends spread quickly throughout the country, some legends remain tightly held secrets whose keepers fear that the mere telling of the secret will somehow diminish its significance. With some trepidation, I decided to contact the local Van Meter library in hopes of finding someone who was still familiar with the legend. I ended up speaking with library director, Jolena Welker, who informed me that the legend of the mysterious beast is still alive among the rural community of Van Meter, and even though many of the specifics of the events had been all but forgotten, much of the original tale had been passed down from generation to generation. At the time, I had no idea that this one phone call would put us on a path to one of the most bizarre and baffling cases that we have ever investigated!

2
Early History of Van Meter
by Chad Lewis

Like many small communities around the county, the town of Van Meter enjoys a rich and interesting history. Long before the first white pioneers made their way to Iowa, the Sac and Fox Tribes were successfully living off the land. The tribes had scattered their bark covered huts along the river, where hunting prey was plentiful and the soil provided bountiful crops. In the early 1840s, the U.S. government signed a treaty with the tribes that effectively took complete control of the land while forcing the tribes to relocate out west. In 1845, brothers Daniel and Lewis Stump noticed the natural richness of the Van Meter area and quickly set about building a cabin on the lush land, making them the first white pioneers in the area to stake out a land claim. Not looking to impress any neighbors, the book *Van Meter Centennial History* described the Stumps' first construction of a permanent structure as being a modest cabin that was "16' x 18' and was one story high."

Levi Wright was one of the first settlers of Van Meter
(Courtesy of the Van Meter Library)

The Stump brothers were followed by another pair of exploring brothers, Levi and James Wright, who also quickly built a cabin on a prime area of land near the fork in the Raccoon River. Soon, other white pioneers started to gobble up the freshly available plots, fields were cleared and planted with crops, cabins were built and renovated, a church was erected, and the once barren landscape slowly began to morph into an early semblance of a community. In 1868, the first passenger train cars of the C.R.I. & P. made their way in to town. The fast growing community of Van Meter was officially laid out in 1869, on land which was owned by a Mr. Wilson, who had been among the first to build a home on the land. Originally known as "Tracy" the town of approximately 450 would eventually change its name to "Van Meter" in honor of J.R. Van Meter, an important early pioneer of the area. Officially incorporated in 1877, the first town-appointed commissioners consisted of J.R. Van Meter, T.E. Moore, G.C. Briggs, W.H. Jennings and B.F. Goar. In 1878, the first mine shaft was sunk and the regular railroad traffic flooded town leaders with dreams of great prosperity and growth. In 1901, to help facilitate the projected growth, the town donated the sum of $2,660 to aid J.R. Van Meter in the construction of a state of the art steam flouring mill. Not everything was smooth sailing, though, as the town took a big hit in 1895 when the mine closed down over continued labor disputes. But even with the mine closed, the town continued to thrive and grow. By 1903, the town was abuzz with nearly 1,000 residents, made up mainly of farmers, tile workers, and small business owners.

3
History of the Brick Factory and Mine
by Chad Lewis

Looking to take advantage of the area's natural resources, plans were drawn up about the possibility of sinking a shaft that could be utilized to mine the untold quantity of coal that was buried deep beneath the land. In 1878, Boag & Van Meter sunk a 257-foot-deep mine down to a three-foot vein. The mine was quickly sold to the Chicago Coal Company who, in 1879, listed their management as:

> J.L. Platt – President
> John Walker – Superintendent
> John Honicker – Clerk
> Ira Hall – Weighboss

Van Meter Coal Mine
(Courtesy of the Van Meter Library)

From the very beginning, the mine put Van Meter on the map. Plenty of passing cargo trains allowed the mine to operate at nearly full capacity without incident. Just as things were starting to really take off, fire reared its ugly head and burned down the main engine house. The *Iowa Geological Survey* reported that "entirely new machinery was installed. Steam hoist was used and machines driven by compressed air were employed for cutting the coal." Soon the Van Meter mine was looked upon as a model for others to replicate. The *Iowa Geological Survey* wrote "This was the first deep mine in the county and for some time was the only one of consequence." In 1879, the fifty men employed at the mine raised 1,000 bushels per day. Again, the *Iowa Geological Survey* reported that "lump coal sold at 9 cents per bushel and nut for eight cents. The Rock Island Railroad Company purchased two flat-car loads, or twenty-six tons daily for use in its engines. The rest of the output was disposed of mostly to local people." Providing overly minute details of the mine, the *Iowa Geological Survey* claimed, "At first both room and pillar and longwall methods of mining were used, but by 1883, the longwall method obtained all through the mine as it proved to be more profitable." In 1893, looking to expand on the success of the mine, the owners decided to establish the Platt Pressed & Fire Brick Company, constructing its building near the mine. The brick factory used red clay from both the mine and the surrounding bluffs to produce high end brick and tile. On February 8, mine and tile factory president J.L. Pratt dropped dead. The New Era wrote that Platt "had been troubled with heart disease for years." More bad news came in 1902, when a work force demanding higher wages and better working conditions went on strike, making it nearly impossible for the management to find workers. Instead of giving in to the workers' demands, the owners simply shuttered the mine for good. The book *Past and Present of Dallas County* put a politically correct spin on the closing by stating, "Owing to the difficulty of securing help and in the increased cost of production, the mine was closed."

Somehow the management of the brick and tile factory was able to distance itself from the employment problems of the mine and continued with uninterrupted production. Production did come to a halt in the fall of 1911 though, when a devastating fire completely destroyed the tile factory. Rather than let the fire ruin their business, the owners looked to re-build the plant as quickly as possible. In the book *Past and Present of Dallas County*, historians claimed that before the charred debris had even fully cooled, motivated workers began clearing out the site in order for construction to begin on a new factory.

Brick and Tile Factory
(Courtesy of the Van Meter Library)

For many decades, the old mine and tile factory has sat on the land of the X family (name withheld) farm and ranch. The multi-generational family still farms and raises livestock on the land—and thankfully kept together several of the old tile buildings, which are still reasonably standing today.

4
Paranormal Beliefs of 1903 Van Meter
by Chad Lewis

In a quest to make a better life in the U.S., many immigrants left behind old friends, family members and prized personal belongings, all in a brazen attempt to flourish in the newfound land of opportunity. This is not to say that the immigrants came here empty-handed. On the contrary, immigrants arrived in the country over-flowing with their superstitions, religious beliefs, rituals, folk remedies, omens and supernatural fears. Many of our greatest paranormal legends were imported by the droves of immigrants flocking to the U.S. Depending on their country of origin, the early settlers would have brought with them stories of ghosts, angels, witches, banshees, demons, sirens, gnomes, vampires, werewolves, sea serpents, and the like. Of course, when these early pioneers first arrived they would have been exposed to the rich culture of the Native Americans, whose long standing legends and beliefs included giant thunderbirds, Wendigo, Sasquatch, water monsters, and an additional assortment of mysterious creatures. (See Chapter 15 - "Early Encounters: Thunderbirds or Thoughtforms?")

No written or oral documentation is available to ascertain the specific beliefs of the first Van Meter residents. The lack of any recorded Van Meter lore forces us to extrapolate beliefs from other similar communities throughout the country. We can also garner a sense of what the pioneers believed in by simply examining the varying types of phenomena that were being reported at the time. We can assume that if there wasn't an underlying belief in the supernatural among the townsfolk, they would not have reported so many paranormal encounters. But the reality was quite the opposite, with tales of the strange and unusual permeating into everyday life, as evidenced by the following cases.

By the early 1900s, the Spiritualist movement, which had fascinated the nation during the mid and late 1800s with the belief that people could communicate with the dead through séances and often unscrupulous psychics, was slowly falling out of fashion, yet stories of ghosts and eerier hauntings continued to amaze and entertain the public. Old newspapers throughout Iowa are chock full of tales of spirits and haunted locations. In Dubuque, inmates were terrified by a ghost haunting the local jail, a mysterious light-wielding spirit spooked countless railroad men as they passed through Waterloo, and in Corwith a mischievous female apparition made a habit of frightening off men as they tried to herd their livestock. Throughout the late 1800s and 1900s, hundreds of similar haunted accounts are littered among the old newspapers and perhaps only account for a miniscule portion of stories that were passed from one generation to another. It is highly likely that Van Meter did not escape the wrath of a good haunted tale; regrettably, if such yarns did exist about people and places of Van Meter, they have been lost to history.

During this period of time science was still in its infancy, and to the general public absolutely anything seemed possible, no matter how outlandish it may have sounded. The idea that some previously unknown species of mysterious animal was out running through the woods, waters, and forests wasn't just fancifully thinking—it was a stark reality. It wasn't until 1902 that scientists "officially" discovered the mountain gorilla in the Virunga Mountains of Africa. In 1903 researchers discerned a slew of new species including a new Madagascar moth (*Xanthopan morganii praedicta*) and an Indonesian Pagai Island macaque.

Not only did people believe that it was possible for mysterious creatures to be roaming the lush jungles and islands of far-flung lands, they also thought they might be lurking in their own backyards. In July of 1903, just two months before the Van Meter encounter, the town of Estherville, Iowa was enthralled over several sightings of a large serpent-like creature inhabiting East Okoboji Lake. The *Estherville Vindicator & Republican* newspaper carried the sensational sightings, claiming that while Mr. and Mrs. Bartlett were out on a fishing excursion they noticed "a terrible commotion in the water. Whatever is was, was moving quite rapidly through the water and quite close to the top, and had the appearance of being as large as an overturned skiff."

1903 Newspaper Article Detailing the Serpent Sighting

Skeptics claimed that it must have been a sturgeon or a misidentification of some other known creature, but the case was never officially solved. Even closer to Van Meter was the growing legend that some Loch Ness type monster was lurking in the waters of the Raccoon River. In her book *Ghosts of Dallas County*, author Lori Pielak collected several accounts of the alleged monster living in the river. Pielak tells of a fisherman who hooked some type of long necked monstrosity that "had a tail like a fish, but a hard shelled body like a turtle," that used large flippers to propel its eight foot long body. Another case revolved around a father and son who were out camping along the river when their peaceful supper was disturbed by a gigantic splash from what at first looked like an alligator. As the beast made another splash, the two campers noticed the beast had "a ripped shell body and long tail," complete with a long neck and teeth. Pielak also interviewed a gentleman whose family had spent generations living along the banks of the Raccoon River. Apparently the family has spotted the creature so many times over the years that it became routine. Similar to other sightings, the man also spoke of the creature's physical makeup being that of a cross between a giant turtle and seal. Whatever the creature is, it seems too cunning to be caught, as many believe it still inhabits the shallow waters of the Raccoon River.

An even more bizarre Iowa legend sprung up around a secluded railroad bridge in the town of Tara, a small community located a few miles outside of Fort Dodge. During the late 1800s the rural railroad bridge was dubbed "Terror Bridge" due to the numerous accounts of it being haunted. Several newspapers of the 1890s reported that "ghost hunters" from Fort Dodge would regularly venture out to the bridge to encounter the ghost, only to leave disappointed. But outside of the ghost stories, another more sinister creature was said to prowl the country side around Terror Bridge. In his book, *Our Lizard Creek Farm*, author Ray Flaherty described a local legend that told of a wild looking man living in the heavily wooded area. This "wildman" was spotted by several residents, but some were convinced that what they saw was certainly no "man." A more recent article by Deann Haden Luke reported that one day a mother, her son and a friend were driving along near Tara when they caught sight of an enormous unknown animal run right past their car at a high speed. They were able to gather a good look at the creature, and what surprised them most was that—whatever it was—it appeared to be a biped, running upright on its hind legs. Since the first sightings of the beast, many other people have witnessed what they thought to be the same exact creature...a mysterious creature the size of a giant bear that was covered with a thick matted down shaggy fur covering its entire body, complete with a long pointed muzzle. The most puzzling aspect to the sightings was the fact that the creature could run effortlessly on its hind legs. For a lack of better description, eyewitnesses began calling it a "werewolf."

Terror Bridge

In the context of such numerous supernatural happenings throughout Iowa, the thought of a small town being terrorized by a large bat-like creature seamlessly flows into the overall belief system of the time. When placed alongside tales of haunted locales, wild hairy bipeds, water serpents and puzzling lights dazzling the skies, the Van Meter Visitor doesn't appear as outrageous as first glace might indicate.

5
1903 Witnesses
by Chad Lewis

Dr. Alcott (Allcott)
First person to fire at the creature

After scouring through historical files, speaking with numerous local historians and reaching out to Van meter residents, we are still left with scarce information about Dr. Alcott. Many of the newspaper accounts mistakenly list him as Dr. A.C. Olcott (Alcott). However, no listing of an "A.C." can be found in the Alcott Van Meter History. There is also some confusion on the correct spelling of Alcott as it has been found spelled as both "Alcott" and "Allcott." When the town re-capped the 1903 incident many years later in an article titled "Posse of Citizens Shoot!", Alcott is listed as "Dr. Fred Alcott." According to local school records, Fred Alcott graduated high school in 1897. An article in the August 27, 1903 edition of the *Malvern Leader* tells of two young Alcott farmers who were accused of stealing pigs. The article states that their parents "are highly respected citizens," of Van Meter. We can assume by the dates that the parents mentioned are also those of Dr. Alcott.

Otto V. White (1868-1952)
His gunshot only seemed to wake the creature up

Several newspapers that covered the story erroneously refer to White as "Dr. O.V. White," which most likely is a mix up with Dr. Alcott. O.V. White was a local businessman who co-owned Fisher & White, a hardware and furniture store on Main Street. In 1905, the Dallas County Census listed him as living with Benjamin Goar (co-owner of the Van Meter Bank). The same census also lists his occupation as "Hardware Merchant." In his article, H.H. Phillips claimed that White was sleeping in one of his rooms above the store when he was awoken by the beast. Being that White owned the hardware store only adds credibility that he was actually sleeping above it as Phillips claimed. While the longevity of the Fisher & White store is not known, it appears that Mr. White continued in the hardware business as evidenced by the 1930 Dallas County Census which also listed his occupation as "Hardware Merchant." Mr. White is buried in the Fairview Cemetery in Winterset, Iowa.

Clarence Dunn "Peter" (1877-1947)
Shot out the bank window

Mr. Dunn was arguably the most widely respected of all the main witnesses. In 1895, Dunn graduated from Adel High School. After high school, he began teaching public school while he continued his academic studies at the Capital City Commercial College, where he graduated in 1901. In 1903, Dunn worked as a cashier for the Van Meter Bank. Over the years, Dunn's trustworthiness and business acumen served him well, and in 1935, when the bank was moved to the nearby town of Adel, Dunn was appointed to Bank Manager. Dunn would continue to operate as the bank's manager from 1935 to 1947. In March of 1947, Dunn's ill heath forced him to retire from his position. Throughout his life in Van Meter, Dunn was the embodiment of the model citizen, serving the community through his various positions of mayor, treasurer, and head of the Van Meter Independent School District. Dunn also found time to be involved as a Scottish Rite Mason, a Knight of Pythias, and a member of the Modern Woodsman of America. In 2012, we interviewed long time Van Meter resident Fletcher Jennings, who was a young man toward the end of Dunn's life. Jennings reiterated the fact that Dunn was considered one of Van Meter's most upstanding citizens and as a man "who ran Van Meter." Mr. Dunn is buried in the Van Meter Cemetery.

Sidney Gregg
Saw the creature climb down a telephone pole

We have uncovered little about the life of Sidney Gregg, including his social stature, profession, family life, and community involvement. The main article listed Mr. Gregg as sleeping in his store, yet the specifics of that store elude us. Nonetheless, it does appear that Mr. Gregg was the proprietor of the store that he occupied. Based on the "Handsome Bachelors" photo, Mr. Gregg does look at bit younger than his colleagues.

J.L. Platt Jr. (1859-?)
Spotted the beast(s) at the old mine

During the time of the sightings, Mr. Platt was in charge of operating the tile plant. The 1905 Dallas County Census listed his occupation as "Coal Mine Director," even though the mines had been closed down for several years prior to the census. The Platt family took control of the mines from Boag & Van Meter. Throughout the years the mine was run by J.L. Platt, J.L. Platt Jr., and finally C.B. Platt.

Ulysses G. Griffith (U.G. Griffith) (1868-1907)
First witness of strange lights

Being the first witness to report the strange activity in Van Meter meant that Griffith's credibility would be heavily scrutinized. At the time of his sighting, Griffith was in his mid-thirties and was highly respected within the region. In 1901 he had teamed up with his brother, David, to purchase an implement, seed and vehicle business, leading to the formation of Griffith Brothers Implement. According to the book *Past and Present Dallas County*, Griffith was "numbered among the leading men of Van Meter, both socially and in a business way and was uniformly respected, for he possessed many good qualities that endured with those whom he came in contact." Griffith also served on the village council and was a proud member of the Masonic Lodge and Modern Woodmen. Historians claimed that "his business integrity was unquestioned and he had a kindly and considerate spirit, which was manifest in geniality and deference for the opinions of others." By all accounts Griffith was a well-respected member of the community "whom the community looked upon as a citizen whom it could ill afford to lose."

H.H. Phillips – Harry H. Phillips
Author of the original creature article

If not for the detailed reporting of Mr. Phillips, the utter terror that accompanied the sudden appearance of the Van Meter Visitor would have been tragically lost to history. Although the exact depths and details of the relationship between Phillips and the rest of the witnesses is only speculative, we can assume they were at the very least acquaintances, based on the "Handsome Bachelors" photo that shows Phillips posing with O.V. White, Sidney Gregg, and U.G. Griffith. In 1900, Phillips served as the Enumerator for the U.S. Census, an important position that would have been given to a trustworthy and capable individual within the community. In 1901, Phillips became the postmaster of Van Meter. A November 5th, 1902 *Des Moines Daily News* article touts Phillips as "a very popular Postmaster" who the residents of Van Meter hope to see "hold the place many years." After Phillips' article was published in 1903, at least one letter was written to both the *Des Moines Daily News* and the *Des Moines Daily Capital* (possibly by the same person) which called into question the credibility of Phillips. However, much like the other witnesses, Phillips was by all accounts a trustworthy and upstanding member of the community.

Secondary Witness

Professor F.L. Martin
Called the beast an antediluvian

Although Professor Martin deemed the creature an "antediluvian," it is unlikely that he actually spotted the creature(s) with his own eyes and based the classification of the creature on descriptions he was given by other witnesses. Professor Martin served as the well-regarded principal of the Van Meter Schools. The *Des Moines Daily News* wrote that Martin was "a school man of marked ability, a graduate of one of the finest colleges in this state and is a man who believes that the manners and morals of the pupils are of the first importance. He believes in thoroughness in scholarship as well as strict discipline and in the years he has been principal he has built up the school greatly." In 1904, Martin withdrew his candidacy for Town Auditor and the *Perry Daily Chief* reported that Martin would also resign as principal "on account of continued poor health." The paper also reported that Martin had plans to leave Dallas County.

6
The Van Meter Visitor:
A Chronology of Events
by Noah Voss

Tuesday - Early Morning - September 29th 1903

There was much to do in 1903 for the well-heeled or at least the daring and adventurous. January premiered the production of *The Wizard of Oz* on Broadway after the wild success of the book release only three years prior. Visitors to Niagara Falls would have been disappointed in March as it ran dry due to the drought sweeping parts of the country. The summer heat did make a great opportunity for a new company by the name of Pepsi to market its product, and if you were lucky enough to pick up one of Ford Motor Company's first cars, the new Model A released in July, you could have even driven to the nearest theater to watch the premier of America's first Western film, *Kit Carson*. The more home-bodied folks living in rural Iowa still could have added color to their night with the brand new product, Crayola crayons, in what must have been a sincerely impressive eight different colors. Much to do indeed, and the weather was cooperating for those who had to spend much of it outdoors.

U.S. Department of Agriculture Voluntary Observers Meteorological Record from September 1903 in Earlham nearby to Van Meter Iowa

It had been a warm start to autumn with just the right amount of rain. Local Van Meter resident U.G. Griffith would have been able to take advantage of the nice weather on Monday to make his rounds, selling different tools through the area. Warm days and cool but comfortable nights are those of light jackets and light discomforts, often affording one the luxury of taking in their surroundings with a relaxed perspective.

As the area's implement dealer, Mr. Griffith must have made this trip countless times for his job. This early Tuesday morning was different. As he pulled into his home town of Van Meter, at the all too often solitary time of 1:00 a.m., he noticed something different. His attention was drawn to the top of Mather & Gregg's building. On the roof was something unusual and out of place—there was a light where there had not ever been one before. As Mr. Griffith continued down the road he drew nearer to the light. He worked through the logical possibilities of what the light could have been. One of his first thoughts was a troublesome one…assuming it might be burglars. As this thought passed into his mind, he cautiously approached closer. Before he was able to draw very near the building something unexpected happened. He must have been relieved yet startled when the light mysteriously moved across the street. It was suddenly clear that he needn't worry about burglars any longer, but he was confounded as to what he had been watching.

The light appeared on the roof of another building, except on the opposite side of the street. His thoughts must have quickened if not his heart with this new observation. "What" he would have wondered to himself, and "how" could something have moved like that? As quickly as the unusual light appeared and mysteriously moved across the street, it simply disappeared all together. Eventually reaching his home in Van Meter, I imagine that Mr. Griffith drifted off to sleep, his mind still circling the unexplained light.

Tuesday - September 29th

What little sleep 35-year-old U.G. Griffith got was likely followed by confused conversation later that day as the town awoke to hear his unusual sighting. They were confused perhaps because Mr. Griffith was an established figure in the community of Van Meter and what's more—respected as a person. With his brother David two years earlier, Ulysses (U.G. Griffith) purchased an implement, seed and vehicle business. Their new enterprise, Griffith Brothers Implement was uniformly respected throughout the Van Meter area. Ulysses G. Griffith was also very active in the community, sitting on the Village Council and a member of at least two local clubs. Newspapers reporting on this sighting insinuate that while perhaps intriguing, U.G. Griffith's sighting did not put the town into a fearful frenzy.

Van Meter Iowa circa 1905. Sign reads "Revolution Store."
(Courtesy of the Van Meter Library)

Something far beyond frenzied fear was to come, and it arrived with fevered fashion the next night. The sun set on Van Meter as any other day. Darkness blanketed the area by 6:30 that evening.

The local town doctor, Dr. Alcott, kept a room in the rear of his office. Thunderstorms rumbled and flashed on the western horizon as Dr. Alcott prepared for bed. Perhaps a dark and stormy night ensued.

Wednesday - Early Morning - September 30th 1903

Hours later, Tuesday evening gave way to earliest parts of Wednesday morning. Outside the early morning's warm southerly winds were kept company by the passing of only the lightest and intermittent rain. Between the clouds and the setting of the moon only 30 minutes prior at 12:27 a.m., it must have been a dark and damp time of the pre-day that was suddenly pierced. In a terrifying moment the doctor was torn from his slumber by a bright light shining in his face. He must have immediately recognized the shock of adrenaline creating his instant alertness. Known as a plucky little fellow, he and his heart raced from bed as his skilled hands wrapped around his nearby "gun of immense proportions."

Historic Van Meter Iowa with street view of early automobile
(Courtesy of the Van Meter Library)

Clearly this was not a light the doctor recognized. He instantly knew no one was seeking his help for a medical emergency or simply stopping by at an odd hour peeking in to see if he was awake—this was different. Wasting no time, and feeling the empowering effects of adrenaline mixed with what must have been annoyance for whomever awoke him, he ran outside the building to confront this conundrum. The ground still wet from the passing showers and the air filled with the familiar smell of freshly fallen leaves, he was challenged with something or other that seemed beyond his years of experience.

Standing behind the source of the light, Dr. Alcott could make out a "half human and half animal" that displayed even more mind boggling traits such as "great bat-like wings." This strange creature before him continued to baffle his racing mind. The doctor could start to see where the light was coming from, and it only muddied the mystery visitor more. In the center of the creature's forehead grew a single blunt horn. The light seemed to be somehow emanating from this blunted horn. The doctor was close to the creature at this point and felt the only course of action was to slay the mysterious and monstrous source of light. Gripping his gun firmly, the doctor fired at the monster. Not only once, or twice to be sure, but five fearful shots were hurled at the beast. He must have had to quickly rethink his initial approach after not even one of the shots had any noticeable effect. With only one remaining shot left, Dr. Alcott quickly retreated back into his office.

Once safe inside, the feeling was fleeting. The doctor quickly locked the doors and frantically moved to do the same to his windows. Sleep was not likely easy to come by and likely with gun in hand, Dr. Alcott eagerly awaited the comfort of light brought on by morning.

Wednesday - September 30th 1903

With such a uniquely unexplainable night, the doctor would have had to share it with someone. Those who heard Dr. Alcott's tale must have had disbelief written on their faces. How could someone such as the town doctor be so trusted with the well-being of others and tell the tale of such terrifying encounters in the darkest of night?

For the rest of Wednesday, Van Meter would have been set abuzz with whispers of Dr. Alcott's nearly harrowing encounter. For those who had heard about Ulysses Griffith's unusual sighting of the acrobatic light the night before, things would have started to add up...but to all the wrong numbers. Van Meter remained cloudy all day, in an almost foreboding gray cast through the otherwise colorful fall foliage.

Street view of Van Meter showing townsfolk with horse and buggy.
Buildings read "Bakery. Restaurant. Groceries." and "dbar Groceries.
Clothing. Hats. Caps.
(Courtesy of the Van Meter Library)

For anyone dismissing the reports out of hand or thinking that the two good chaps just had a bad dinner, more witnesses were to be created…and in short order.

The sun had now long since set on Wednesday and the moon peered out from behind the mostly cloudy nighttime sky.

Thursday - Early Morning - October 1st 1903

Though mostly cloudy skies blanketed the hamlet of Van Meter throughout the early morning hours, on Thursday was the first sighting to take place with the moon still having not yet set. One can imagine our next brave soul, Clarence Dunn, as he walked alone through the quiet night. Clarence was known to his friends as Peter, though he was only kept company this evening by a silent and just-a-sliver-more-than-a-half moon peering out between passing clouds. Shadows began to be illuminated by the soft glow of the moon, only to be suddenly swallowed up by the dimmest dark of the next passing cloud. This give and take of illumination must have seemed more menacing to Peter tonight than any other…. a short and soundless battle taking place all around him between the light and the dark with each passing cloud. Even with other people around here and there, these are the thoughts that can attack an aware man's calm. Peter was on a steadfast mission and would not be deterred.

Peter was widely respected and graduated high school from a neighboring town. After completing his collegiate studies, he took a job as the cashier for the Van Meter Bank. So respected by his neighbors, Peter would be promoted to bank manager and hold several city positions, including mayor, over the next few decades. Tonight, however, he was simply a man, alone in the dark, who had left the safety of his home and family to watch over the bank. Every next footstep, hushed by the growing layer of damp, dead leaves.

Peter had feared robbers were perhaps the source of all the town's excited sightings and was determined to introduce them to his committed character. To help steady his nerves, he carried his "trusty shot gun" packed with a formidable load of buckshot. Once at the bank, Peter settled in for a long night's watch. Just as on the previous two nights, things started to occur right around 1:00 a.m. The town clock struck one when he heard another noise—one he had not expected.

The noise was confusing. Was it that of garbled gasps for air by some unseen creature whether wild animal or human? Peter thought that it was perhaps "some one [sic] strangling," but before he could investigate further or listen longer a "mysterious light shone full upon him through the front window." The light was revealed so sudden and bright that Peter was almost blind. The light snapped off of him in what must have been a huge, if not momentary, relief. As the light moved, it darted about the room and Peter was able to garner a better glimpse of the source. As his eyes began to relax, a "great form of some kind" began to reveal itself. Just as suddenly as the light darted about the room, almost scanning, it swung back to him once more. Peter's nerves could stand it no longer; steadying the barrel of the shotgun towards the creature, he fired point blank. In his haste, he did not give chase to the outside or even open the window, but out of such stymied shock Peter's shot shattered the glass and part of the sash. Then nothing.

As quickly as the light appeared, the creature disappeared. A more thorough search was made as soon as dawn broke six long hours later. Peter thought he had killed the creature but nothing remained, save a few tracks. In true modern day cryptozoologist form, Peter even made a plaster cast of the "great three-toed tracks."

The Van Meter Bank as printed on their windows shown with two men
(Courtesy of the Van Meter Library)

As the rest of Van Meter awoke and began their normal daily routine, it is understandable for witnesses to subjugate unexplained things that came from the shadows occurring in the dead of night. An experiencer might try to convince themselves it was something it didn't seem to be. Another might simply be too stressed with the job or preparing the next meal to invest any more time in fanciful obscurities.

Thursday brought many a normal thing to distract one's mind, such as the first game of the very first modern World Series. The Boston Americans pitted against the Pittsburgh Pirates to help kick off the modern franchise. Even in the sometimes isolated Midwestern woods of Iowa, such Americana culture would have occasionally taken center stage. The terrifying things that can happen in the dark of night can be forgotten in the light of day and the company of others—but only for a time.

Though it was clear skies and sunshine just to the south for most of the day Thursday, the clouds hung almost meaningfully around Van Meter as if knowing there would be something more to obscure. The sun would set in nine fleeting hours, and darkness would again drip down across the land…and with it, something else.

Thursday Evening - October 1st 1903

Soft winds brought a wispy rain slowly from the north, just enough to dampen the bones a bit on this forlorn autumn evening. The town slowly quieted down as the daily to-do's got done or put off until Friday.

Things were quiet until the very striking moment a grating, sharply harsh and pointed noise broke the night's stillness. O.V. White was jolted awake by this abrupt "rasping" racket emanating from just outside his second-story room on Main Street. He kept lodgings over the Fisher & White hardware and furniture store that he co-owned. Mr. White wasted no time in arming himself, likely hearing the talk of some mysterious monster terrorizing the town at night. He may have already had a good idea of what he was in for when he grabbed his gun and moved towards his window. The noise was so scraping on his spirit that he quickly opened his window and peered out into the darkness and rain for what gave birth to such a bewildering clatter. Then there was nothing.

As Mr. White's eyes adjusted to the night, he detected a dark figure on the cross member of the telephone pole. It took only a moment and Mr. White believed he was staring right at the monster.

The Van Meter train depot
(Courtesy of the Van Meter Library)

Scarcely 15 feet away, the now determined Mr. White "took deliberate aim" and, as with any good marksman, in one slow exhale he pulled the trigger and fired. The creature did not fall to the ground as the "ordinarily…good shot" Mr. White was expecting. Instead, at the very moment he fired instantly its light was turned on him. The shot from his gun didn't have any effect on the creature other than to "waken it up." His heart had to jump at this terrifying realization—he may have no way to defend himself from this monster. Mr. White recalled a powerful "odor" suddenly filling the air. The odor was emitted from the monster, according to Mr. White, and was so strong that it "seemed to stupefy him." Oddly enough, in an experience already past capacity for unusual, he could remember "no more about" the night. As the shot rang out, it awoke neighbor Sidney Gregg. Gregg, torn from his slumber, raced towards his door to see what the commotion was about.

As he opened the door and peered towards Main Street, he was met with the most curious creation descending the telephone pole. Mr. Gregg was afforded a different view of the creature as he was sleeping in his store that is just across the corner from where O.V. White had viewed the monster from. Mr. Gregg watched on in dumbstruck disbelief as the "monster" descended the telephone pole after the manner of a parrot, using its huge beak. Upon reaching the ground it stood erect, and by Mr. Gregg's estimates it was "at least eight feet high." Whatever it was, the light from its forehead was as "bright…as an electric headlight." The light again darted about just as it had the nights before when the Visitor came to see Peter Dunn and Dr. Alcott seemingly in a "searching" motion. Mr. Gregg could have been under a more diluted daze than that of O.V. White from the cryptic stench, but he continued to watch on doing his best to process this entirely baffling being even as it flapped its great featherless wings. With the flapping of its wings the creature took giant "leaps" almost like that of a kangaroo. Just then, as if an answer to a silent question racing through Mr. Gregg's mind, *"Am I dreaming?",* the fast mail came tearing through town right on schedule. This train on nearby train tracks made its own familiar racket to the townsfolk in Van Meter. To the creature standing a mere 15 feet from Mr. Gregg, this seemed to be an unfamiliar noise—it responded to the train's presence when it "crouched as if in a spring." The creature paused only for a moment, because it then sprang up and "ran on all four feet" heading toward the old coal mine. The creature with "wings extended…sailed away" and disappeared. Mr. Gregg, clearly flustered by the inexplicable nights events, only then remembered he had a gun, but it was too late to use it.

If the Van Meter Visitor remained in the area for anyone to see the rest of the night, no one did. A change was on the wind.

Friday - October 2nd 1903

Friday had a wet start, though it would have only taken the slightest rain to dampen the people's spirit and perhaps their perspective on the escalating events to come. To be sure, the once whispers of unusual events cloaked in the dark of night surrounding Van Meter were now conversations raised to full argument volume throughout the town. Friday would have been a clear apex in the shift of any conversations. By this time they must have all been discussing the mysterious Visitor.

A visitor comes calling in the middle of the night as you sleep. It is immense in size, towering above the tallest and strongest in town, and bullets seem to have no effect. No longer would have the "confused witness" been an acceptable excuse, but now a more pointed problem of "what is really going on here" would come across most people's lips as more plea than question. This is where the fear lies—the unknown. At the end of lengthy conversations that explored all angles of explanation between sips of coffee. Discussing each data point in every sighting over lunch and over again after. Seeking out the trusted opinion of those who find themselves on a pedestal in Van Meter merely to be met with raised shoulders, shaking heads and excuses thinly veiled as explanations. Professor Martin of Van Meter's South Side High School pronounced the visitor as "some sort of an antediluvian monster."

Artist interpretation of a more antediluvian Van Meter Visitor potential
(Artwork by Kevin Lee Nelson)

Only after all the theories that don't fit have been put forward and all the questions that remain are growing larger than one person can remember, then—and only then—does fear start to spread. Even if the town's folk don't know what it is they need to fear, or if they should at all, they begin to see it everywhere they look. People see fear in each other's eyes over the rim of their pint glass. The distracted eye on the approaching twilight coloring the far horizon is a clue to the internal discomfort. It can be seen in the wrapping up of chores early and the extra lights illuminating each house. The fear of the unknown grows as one's powerlessness becomes more clear and the twilight more dim. The fear in one's mind is often far more cavernous than the cause before the eyes—though in Van Meter on this day that just may not be so.

Wilson Street Van Meter Iowa. Building reads "Manbeck" and below
townsfolk on walkway
(Courtesy of the Van Meter Library)

Friday Evening - October 2nd 1903

The townsfolk watched a thunderstorm rumble, roll and flash in the west with much the same trepidation they did the sun setting and with it the start of another terrifying night. Nightfall would bring with it darker shadows than most in Van Meter would remember them being. Much had changed in just a week and, though the shadows had not, they were now large enough in which things could no longer lurk, but did—things that over the last four frightful nights have removed themselves from the forgettable obscuration of one's nightmares and into the streets of Van Meter. The creature had revealed itself to many already.

Sadly for the scared, monsters were no longer confined to their minds— even the shadows—as the men at the mine located on the edge of town had new reports. The work crews at the mine area were manned both day and night. They had been hearing noises for some time emanating from the mine shafts. Not just noises mind you, but only the sounds that the most fearful mind can hear reported as "though Satan and a regiment of imps were coming forth for a battle." The uproar of commotion would continue until reaching a fever pitch only an hour into Saturday morning. It would be a restless night for those catching wind of the newest monster reports.

*View of Van Meter Tile & Brick Factory on the grounds of the old mine
(Courtesy of the Van Meter Library)*

Saturday - Early Morning - October 3rd 1903

The old coal mine on the edge of town had been shut down a few years prior to the unusual events of the past week in Van Meter. There was, however, a functioning tile and brick factory on the same grounds, and operations manager J.L. Platt, Jr. was there this early Saturday morning. The rain still decided ever so often to start and stop, as well as the mysterious noises emanating from the old mine shafts. As 1:00 a.m. approached almost as on cue, the sounds from the mine shaft drew J.L. Platt, Jr. to the edge. The moon was nearly full and, when not obstructed by the passing rain clouds, would have afforded Mr. Platt, Jr. to peer down just a bit further into the dark borehole. These mine shafts can drop down hundreds of feet with many twists and turns off in every direction or a straight drop with no turns at all. Often times there can be a hundred foot drop or more to a bitterly cold and blindingly dark water column that not only can be another hundred feet deep, but also polluted with the worst runoff and chemical concoctions from when the mine was active. Add to that the deadly gasses that can fill them and either explode with the slightest spark or silently suffocate anyone foolish enough to draw so near as to fall in. J.L. Platt, Jr. was used to these mine shafts, and as he drew near the eerily familiar sounds they were faint no longer. The echo of "Satan" and the "imps" was in full chorus, still preparing for the forthcoming battle. This time however, the disturbing sounds did not stop and in the flash of a moment the monster appeared at the entrance. The shocking moment was not over, as directly behind the first monster there appeared another somewhat smaller one. They both gave off the "brilliant light" that was as striking as it was blinding. J.L. Platt, Jr. would have been just one of many witnesses to the creatures, as all the men working the tile and brick factory were nearby some "40 rods" or about 660 feet away. A few of the braver, however, would have likely approached the mine entrance behind J.L. Pratt, Jr. Mr. Pratt did have a good look at the monsters as they flew past, noticing their horn-like protuberance emanating the extraordinary light as they "sailed" away into the dark. As chilling as this experience may have been for the men present, they took comfort in their accidental discovery that could rid them and the town of Van Meter from the monsters—they had just discovered their lair.

This latest sighting at the mine shaft would have spread speedily through town, even at the odd hour. Men gathered their brimmed hats and rain coats for protection from the rain as they hatched a hasty and nefarious plan of ambush for the monsters. They geared up with their most trusted, if not largest, gun available and headed back out into the night. As they left the sturdy confines of their homes, all the electric lights were turned on. Indeed, as they moved through the town back to the old mine and as word spread, the lights all over town were turned on in hopes to offer those left behind some protection and to frighten the monsters off. Should the creatures return to the old mine opening, a crowd of men and guns were gathered together near the entrance. Their plan was simple: "to rid the earth of them when they should return." Then the waiting began.

The cooler temperatures, pared with the dank drizzle, can wear on a man's spirit. After the excitement or at least adrenaline diminishes, the polish of any initial plan wears off and makes this time the hardest part of any plot. It is vital to keep your focus on the mission—stay not just awake but alert, for here there be monsters. And wait they did, at least four hours with nothing but their thoughts and what must have been nervously whispered conversations.

Nothing returned to the old mine area through the night, even though the watch never wavered. Just when the depression of defeat was starting to seep into the psyche of the men, someone noticed something. Perhaps it was the breaking of dawn at 5:46 a.m. and the warm comforting colors that began to return to the sky that allowed the dark figured, eight-foot-tall creature with huge, bat-like wings to be spotted as it approached the old mine. Not far behind was the second creature sighted a few hours earlier. The men who were still gathered at the mine fired shots. In a moment, their considerable guns fired countless times at the beasts. It must have sounded like an explosion erupting from the mine area to the rest of Van Meter now just slumbering awake in their homes, beds still warm. It is recounted that the "reception received would have sunk the Spanish fleet." The creatures added to the chaotic situation with their own thunderous and "unearthly noises" in response to the bullets. Then the peculiar odor returned as if released from the monsters. The men who laid in wait would have sent bullets down range to the monsters as fast as they could shoot. The same men were forced to watch in bewildered trepidation as the unaltered monsters casually and slowly descended the shaft of the old mine. As the last man fired his last bullet, I imagine a surreal silence befalling the entire grounds of the factory.

Such boisterous noise and carnage of explosions only a moment before causes a certain veil to fall over such men's senses. They become sharpened in one regard, with narrowed and focused vision. Often the hearing may dull and you don't feel your toes in your boots the same way you did just a moment before. As the extreme moment passes, these simple things that you were oblivious to only a moment prior become obvious again, as does the fact that you lost them for a time. Once the men realized that despite their most sincere and best efforts they had not accomplished their goal, something else creeps back in—fear. Some respond with excited conversations, dissecting the events as they happened only a moment before, just as on any big game hunt. The less emotional men would have had some realization that can rattle a person to their core; though they would likely never utter the words aloud, the new insight happens all the same. Whether they knew it or not, the men were powerless and even more confused than the day before. The once warriors would have begun to disperse.

View of Van Meter from the Tile & Brick Factory and
grounds of the old mine
(Courtesy of the Van Meter Library)

Heading off to begin work for the day, maybe back to finish the half started chores, or perhaps if they were lucky back to the preferred familiarity of their home and warmth of family. The group of defeated men trudged through town slowly breaking off of the group to head their own way. Confused conversations, sentences started but never finished, extinguishing the lights that gave them comfort only a few hours ago as they headed out to slay the beast terrorizing their town. The men were now forced to balance the new reality that held monsters with their old beliefs. For some it is easiest and even an unconscious task to simply push that part of your mind down into a place where you are not forced to think of it again. For others, coming to terms is more complicated.

Saturday - October 3rd 1903

As the tale of the terrorizing events at the factory and old mine undoubtedly burned through town like an uncontrollable wild fire, action needed to be taken. If only talking about action, to quell the fear before it built to full scale panic, it was still needed. The town is all excitement and a "force of men has been set to work to barricade the mouth of the mine." A logical response to what seems to be a creature that calls the mine home during the day and is impervious to bullets in the night. Locking up the monster in the mine like a cage seems like a good next step for those wanting to quickly and quietly place the previous week's events into the forgotten history of Van Meter. The townsfolk discussed several methods of exterminating the monsters but nothing seems to meet the approval of those in charge.

From here we are left to wonder even more blindly. Did they get the mine opening barricaded before nightfall? If so, did the creatures find another way out, or are their skeletons still deep inside the mine to this day? Perhaps not affected by bullets, they too do not feel the cold, careless grip of time and are still trapped there today, evermore exploring for an exit? Maybe the determined residents of Van Meter decided on pursuing another course, one of more drastic extermination? Or was nothing done and the monsters simply never appeared in the area again? The first printed account of events was likely written by resident H.H. Phillips. I envision him frantically scratching paper strewn out before him under the dim light of a flickering candle. Rushed to tell the world of what had been happening in Van Meter with the hopes that someone might be able to help them with their monster infestation. Phillips perhaps made his way to send off the letter before sundown that very Saturday on his way to meet up with the group of locals hatching what they all hoped to be the final plan for the Van Meter Visitor. The reporter himself not yet sure on how the developing story would unfold.

We have not yet found another H.H. Phillips authored article about the Visitor. Perhaps his initial article is held now as the last free word written telling the tale. Maybe the monsters returned with a vengeance, remaining passive no more. The creatures so tired of the relentless tirade of bullets that the very next sunset they attacked and lay control over the once uncontrolled people of Van Meter. The first article appeared in the *Des Moines Daily News* the following day, Sunday October 4th, 1903. Was there nothing more ever written by H.H. Phillips about the end for this mysterious monster? Is that because there was nothing more to say? Perhaps something new came with the creatures at nightfall and changed the people so they no longer wanted their story told. The people placed under some advanced scientific technology or mythical magic mechanism. The people no longer of their own volition to vehicle their bodies about as they desired, but under the control of something more sinister. The residents forced to do some foreign bidding and forget. This, of course, is a bit of fanciful fun more fitting for the Van Meter Visitor film's twist ending.

Perhaps more answers will turn up as more people hear about the strange sightings around Van Meter in 1903. Maybe Phillips did write another article that detailed the following week offering the least bit of closure. If so, the end of the story may have not been deemed fit by the newspaper for printing. Perhaps the second week of events was non-existent, or better still—so sensational it was even more unbelievable. Maybe the answers lie in dusty boxes forgotten in the attic of some distant relative of Phillips. If there ever was a plaster cast, it would be glorious for it to turn up, though difficult to authenticate. It's possible that a dark, dank basement of some home in Van Meter holds an album, sandwiched between its lonely pages the rest of the story.

THEORIES

7
Cryptozoological Derivations: Exploring the Possible Connection to Countless Other Creature Sightings
by Noah Voss

When looking at other reports of mysterious and unexplained creatures from around the world there were two chief qualifications that I was seeking. One: in a simple world it would be clearly confirmed that as the creature was no longer reported in Van Meter, it was beginning to get reported in another, stop and then repeat in another. This, of course, didn't happen. Had it, that would have been a huge step forward in creating a profile of the Visitor. These are normal results while researching the paranormal field. Of course, this assumes that the Visitor doesn't have somewhere to hideout where there are no humans. No humans mean no one to document and report that sighting.

More to the first point, it is possible the creature was sighted elsewhere, but simply not documented or recorded anywhere that I could ever find. From there, of course, we could then move into the more obscure and complicated potentials…perhaps the Visitor has places other than the Earth in which it can travel to. If not other places, perhaps this creature is not constrained by simple linear time and is able to not only travel to other places but other times. As you can see, this speculation all becomes a bit of a Pandora's box. Much can be discussed, much less can be verified.

The second qualification I focused on while searching for similar unexplained creature sightings was more a state of being—objectivity. It is imperative that any investigator remain objective while examining and collecting data. Remaining conscious that your focus is not exclusively on the data that fits your theory can be difficult for even the most seasoned investigator. To get tunnel vision seeking data that supports one's belief system—at the risk of ignoring the data that does not—is a sure way to make false progress with your theory. In addition, to blindly assume that there was no contaminating of the reports from the witnesses' own belief system would be an error. Witnesses have beliefs that can make them more likely to witness any event one way over another. People's belief systems are naturally colored by their past experiences. To include this data in your theory with too high a value is to perform a disservice to your efforts.

What can we safely speculate from more than 100 years away about the belief system of the Van Meter area witnesses? Well, if they had read a dime store novel about the Spring Heeled Jack (which was in wide circulation around 1903), that may or may not have affected how they wholly perceived the experience. The Spring Heeled Jack was a mysterious being, sighted for decades throughout Great Britain and beyond. He characteristically was described as humanoid but had dazzling lights, featherless wings and even a putrid scent. In reality there were many other repeating characteristics that would show a clear difference from the Van Meter Visitor such as being far more humanoid than beastly, wearing clothes and often a striped shirt and no single horn. An additional example arises from 1868 when there was a large wave of unexplained things being witnessed. They were labeled the Chilean Dragon sightings and were heavily written about in North American papers. Again, we see by 1873 flying dragons had been reported through Texas and Kansas garnering some national coverage. Then 1882 brought the publication of flying crocodile sightings through California. In 1886 there were a few flying amphibious monster sightings published in papers from reports documented years earlier. Then in 1890 Tombstone, Arizona, had a unique flying pterodactyl-like sighting wave that got picked up in newspapers. It is fairly certain that at least some of the Van Meter residents had read about these events. What the exact results were on the witnesses is probably as varied as the potential effect.

Whether the area's populace had these aged stories on the tip of their tongue or the front of their mind we may never know. This becomes part of the huge number of variables to wade through. These past stories may or may not affect the people equally depending on the person's state of mind or life experiences. Perhaps exposing one's subconscious is enough to make a lingering difference in how you later—even decades later— interpret unusual sightings in the dark of night or break of dawn. Then again, perhaps it is not.

Let me be clear on one thing: I currently believe, based on my travels, that having these general encounters may at most color an experience only slightly. I further believe that if this is the case, it is so only for some people. I do not feel that these passing encounters with the written word carry enough influence with them to cause large scale misidentifications of more mundane events. For me, this is not an explanation of the Van Meter Visitor. They did not simply read about something mysterious and then misidentify a turkey vulture as the Van Meter Visitor. To say so, is a clear indication that one has not reviewed all the data.

So we discussed our research and investigation into what the Van Meter Visitor could have been misidentified from. The potential for misidentification is always a possibility worth exploring and we dutifully cut our way through native or not so native birds and bats both. I feel fairly confident that there is no known source, native or otherwise, that would clearly explain away the mystery that surrounds the Van Meter Visitor.

Let's look at another way of attacking this mystery then.

Since it happened in 1903, we won't likely come up with any new or additional data surrounding any specific Van Meter event. Hopefully more information will become revealed at some point in the future, but for now we are left with what we have. We are left to move forward assuming that the majority of the first-hand eyewitness observations from multiple people, over numerous days, are mostly correct instead of mostly wrong. If we are to construct more theories, we are going to need more data. Was anyone else in the Midwest seeing anything similar to the Visitor? Perhaps even further out, since we don't know what we're dealing with? Indeed, to assume a small area of habitat or travel may be as inane as assuming a large one. The answer is yes, people were seeing odd and mysterious creatures throughout the country in and around the time of 1903.

Reported oddities such as horns or great height and immense wingspan estimates are cause for inclusion and further research. Not that their mere sighting alone proves anything, but it may begin to allow for the additional data to reveal the ever elusive but always promising trends that create useful profiles. It is very important that working theories be built upon actual data points, even if circumstantial eyewitness observations.

I aimed to include cryptid type sightings that had 3-4 or more similar characteristic traits to the Van Meter Visitor. These characteristics were from first-hand eyewitness descriptions of any observable traits such as: physical characteristics (i.e. bat-like wings or light emanating), physical movements (i.e. moving on all fours or climbing with the assistance of a "beak"), known habitat (i.e. caves or mines), time of appearance (i.e. always at night or always after midnight) and finally surrounding potentially related events (i.e., does a death always follow a sighting or does a natural disaster likely follow a sighting).

During my research for subsequent investigations into the Van Meter area and this section of the book, I was able to compile a list of more than 50 unusual reports from around the world that held some similarities to our Visitor. I will focus further on those reports that are documented before modern times to help rule out more uncertain variables—predominantly hoaxes. For time and clarity sake, let's look in brief detail on the following four reports that hold some similar characteristics to that of the Van Meter Visitor.

The Lake Elizabeth's Area Sighting

The Lake Elizabeth's (Elizabeth's Lake) California creature sightings are sure to wow. There are many descriptions and many questions that surround the validity of this reported creature. In 1918 author Horace Bell, in his book *On The Old West Coast*, discusses his questions but also documents older legends from original Mexican settlers. They, too, had told of mysterious creatures through what would become Elizabeth's Lake. It is purported that the Spanish priest Junipero Serra had said a pet of the Devil called the lake home in 1780. Later the newspapers documented sightings from the 1830s through 1886 that included such descriptions as a flying alligator with six legs and twelve bat-like wings.

Newspaper account of the creature at Lake Elizabeth

1902 Baltimore Snallygaster Sightings

The half-bird and half-reptile creature was named by the predominantly German settlers in the 1730s. In their native tongue they named the mysterious creature *Schneller Geist* (Quick Spirit). Much like this creature's reported varying features, the name is now more commonly known as The

Snallygaster to locals. The Snallygaster's long "metallic beak" is said to be lined with "razor" looking teeth. There were also reports of odd noises associated with the Snallygaster such as metallic machinery sounds perhaps similar to the Van Meter Visitor rasping noises. It calls the Blue Ridge Mountains in Maryland home, though it has been reportedly witnessed in surrounding states over the years. The Snallygaster's immense wings may have allowed it to snatch victims up into the sky, sucking them dry of blood, or so the legends spoke of. There was a surge in reported sightings of the Snallygaster in 1902, including numerous livestock deaths blamed on the beast. With fear on the rise, the locals of that time responded with how their belief system allowed, by placing large hex signs on their barns. In their culture it was believed that these large six sided stars would offer protection from the beast that attacked in the night—The Snallygaster.

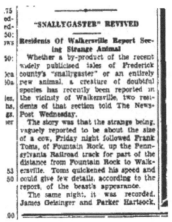

A circa 1903 newspaper account of the Snallygaster sightings

The Jersey Devil

The infamous Jersey Devil or Leed's Devil has a long history of sightings throughout the New Jersey area of the United States. Indeed, by some accounts the sightings may span centuries, but even in the most conservative documentation reports range from the 1800s up through today. Oddly enough, by most accounts there were no reports of the Jersey Devil between 1903 and 1909. Perhaps the Jersey Devil grew tired of the area and visited Van Meter in the autumn of 1903, only to move on shortly after to points unknown. When the sightings picked back up in New Jersey, researchers today estimate that there were a reported 1,000 witnesses or more that year alone. While the Jersey Devil doesn't match every reported characteristic of the Van Meter Visitor, it does have several similar common descriptors worth discussing. Of course, as with any legend that holds sightings spanning centuries, one is bound to have a wide and colorful data pool of descriptions to draw from.

If we look at the more often-used descriptors, we find some similarities such as bat-like wings, active at night, the ability of flight and four legs that would allow Van Meter witnesses to observe that their creature "ran on all four feet with wings extended." The Jersey Devil is often described with wings off of the back and arms in front which would allow for normal mechanics of extending the wings while at the same time moving on all fours. What isn't similar, or at least not consistent, is the description of the creature's feet. At times it is reported as having claws, which may help for comparisons to the three-toed print found in Van Meter. While other times the Jersey Devil is seen with great hooves. While the Van Meter Visitor is consistently reported as having a beak and horn, the Jersey Devil ranges from a horse head, more bird or pterodactyl-like, to that of a dragon-headed monster. Obviously, the horse head reports would make it a stretch for any direct comparisons to our Iowa Visitor. But there are other observations are not that far off. To look at the Van Meter Visitor, the Jersey Devil, or any other mysterious creature sightings on this list with such basic comparison points may be to oversimplify an overtly complicated set of different events to the detriment of our research.

Eyewitness account of the Jersey Devil sighting in old newspaper

How torturously complex must the theories then become? We may be potentially dealing with some event being witnessed by people who quite literally do not have the biological capacity to understand said events. This potential demands extremely intricate models indeed. Not that the witnesses themselves are exceptionally dim, rather that which is being observed cannot be comprehended by humans. If that is the case, or even remotely close to reality (ours or another's), then the changing of physical characteristics becomes one of the least strange items. Believe it or not, there is much science behind this very idea of alternate dimensions and what may lie there.

Most grasp the first three dimensions. I know I had felt that way, only to discover as I learned more about the models revealing the additional dimensions that I had to expand my understanding of even the first three. However, beginning with the fourth dimension and above, there is a uniquely complex intertwining that, among many other things, can help show potential in our Van Meter Visitor case. Chiefly to our point the potential sources offered in the different dimensions. These dimensions— that number up to 11 in the more popular mathematical models—create the very real potential of visitors from other dimensions.

To look at our Van Meter Visitor descriptions changing another way, we could get simpler instead of complex. Maybe each Visitor was different; after all, they weren't wearing name tags. Indeed even the converse possibility that the same "being" was being sighted or that each sighting was a different "being" cannot be ruled out. After all, not all humans on Earth look the same, while others appear identical. The additional variables and potentials to consider with this complicated view on reality are incalculable for most. If you need to place this potential of visitors from other dimensions as a whimsical mental exercise until you can approach it with a cool head and hot cup of coffee, do so…but please do revisit. This can quickly become overwhelming and, as a result, off-putting. We are delving far beyond our belief system here. What each witness may prefer to observe, or even compared to what each of these strange visitors from elsewhere project when interacting with someone here, only adds to the mountain of variables. As implied, this is only the beginning of a very long, twisty and currently dangerously dark rabbit hole that Kevin attempts to illuminate a bit in his ultraterrestrial section.

for a long time paralyzed with fear, not

Artist re-creation that appeared in newspaper featuring the Stansbury Island Creature

The Stansbury Island Creature

The Stansbury Island creature sighting is wrought with contradictions. Some inconsistencies are understandable; others flirt with fanciful. This area of Utah in early September 1903 was the backdrop for two hunters' wild encounter with the unknown. An intriguing adjunct is the date of their experience…just three weeks before Van Meter Iowa would have its Visitor sightings. As reported by newspapers of the time, two witnesses, Martin Gilbert and John Barry, were hunting "over the island" when they first report seeing the "half bird and half reptile." They were able to study the habits of the creature "for three days" including its wings being "bat-like." The paper waxes on about the likely antediluvian source for such a "prehistoric species." Witnesses report a description combining that of a "fish, alligator and bat," but the qualities get even one step beyond bizarre when given length estimates. It is reported that "Gilbert places its length at 50 feet," though his co-witness estimates longer. When compared to the Van Meter Visitor, the reported size does not match. It is more data, however, for us three writing this book to build onto theories born of our lifetime of researching. One comparable characteristic of this creature are the "fiercely glowing" eyes which could at least be similar to the blinding light later reported as emanating from the Van Meter Visitor. The creature's immense size allowed it to carry a horse to a cave on Stansbury Island as the two nearby hunters listened to the creature consuming the meal. Of course, here we can see potential similarities as the Van Meter Visitor seemed to frequent the town's mine just as the Stansbury creature sought the safety of a cave

As hinted with the potential ultraterrestrial theory, all the rules might be summed up best with just one: there are no rules that we know of. This rule is not conventionally helpful, however very nurturing when brainstorming the pre-model stage of the scientific method. Sadly, free-associating is something that the paranormal field is not short of. More to that ultraterrestrial point with this case, it is imperative to look at exactly what Gilbert was reported as saying in the papers:

"...when suddenly to the northwest there appeared a thing. I don't know what to call it. It looked to me like a brilliant rainbow folded into compact mass, moving rapidly through the air."

Wow...a lot and nothing to go with there all at the same time. Assuming that this entire sighting is not a piece of fiction, it is interesting to me how similar some aspects of the witnesses experiences mirror those of more common unexplained reports I've investigated. There are parts that it seems like a UFO sighting, or someone on Skinwalker Ranch, which is also in Utah. The Skinwalker Ranch has had countless mind bending reports such as watching a mysterious looking "doorway" open in the middle of the air, only to have shadows and lights come through from what appears to be another time or place. I have personally investigated a region in Wisconsin with just such a legend. Annaton is a very rural area with a big mystery known to only a few. It is rumored that every so often people witness some sort of doorway open up on the sides of the bluffs. Through this portal it appears to be a different time of day and perhaps a different time era. Even if the entire sighting on Stansbury Island proves to be false, the opportunity to make a valid if not intricate point remains. It would be easy to view such experiences as magic or the experiencer as crazy. Notwithstanding, I feel it is conceivable that we are dealing with some as yet unknown phenomena that may one day be explained in part or in full by applying the scientific method. These observed events, as unusual as they may seem now, in the future could be determined to be a natural state of the universe we live in or controlled by other intelligence.

There are times on my adventures where no amount of talent could describe the events that have occurred in any realistic vein, because I feel they deal with alternative realities that we have yet to fully comprehend. When presented in the wrong way or in the wrong context, the people involved can look foolish at best. At worst, they may inaccurately seem downright psychotic or outright crafting the whole experience themselves. This all has been said before in many ways by those who go looking into the strange and unexplained for any length of time. From outside of the paranormal field, and even to many in the field of study, this ultraterrestrial model can seem like a lazy response to complicated data. I, myself, may have held such beliefs in my younger years, only to become one of those researchers decades later seemingly walking around an invisible answer, pointing the whole time, telling people it is right there in front of them. To my perhaps unique life experiences, it seems like Gilbert of the Stansbury Island Creature sighting may simply be a person attempting to speak about an experience for which we have no language. Whenever that is seemingly the case, it has further been my experience that the listener, attempting to comprehend what is being communicated, may find it easier to dismiss the experience and the experiencer as irrational and wrong. Herein lies my challenge to you, the reader. Remain objective above all else, but also challenge your beliefs no matter how objectively obtained. Be willing to evolve, change, remove and replace part or all of your belief system when introduced to new applicable data. Do not dismiss possibility because it is unfamiliar or difficult. Relegate that which you have determined unlikely to that category only after you have sincerely and objectively reviewed all available data.

There was a sort of precedents set for this Great Salt Lake event surrounding the Stansbury Island, whether the area residents knew in 1903 or not.

There were documented sightings of creatures in and around the lake in 1877 and three decades prior to that. Looking even further back into the oral traditions of the native peoples of the area reveals the Giant Mosquito Monster. The problem, among many, is that even looking at the whole picture doesn't prove anything. The anecdotal data of previous sightings in the area does not demonstrate proof either for the existence of a mysterious creature nor in the existence of a fictitious article published in the newspaper. Quantifiable and verifiable data is difficult to come by in more modern investigations, let alone researching cases from more than a century earlier. So what can we learn today from more modern data that may apply to our Van Meter case in 1903? It brings us to a slightly more tangible potential source of the Van Meter Visitor.

The National Science Foundation has a project focusing in part on flora and fauna population estimates. Their "Tree of Life" project estimates that in addition to the 1.7 million identified and known species on the planet Earth, there may be as many as 100 million in total. That's a big number of species on this planet and only a small percentage of them identified. Add to that the sobering statistic from the United Nations Environment Programme that estimates 73,000 species become extinct—annually. That is more than an estimated 800,000 species extinct since the 1903 Visitor sightings. How many of those species that are gone forever were never even documented? Perhaps the last two of a lost species were witnessed around Van Meter in 1903? One might additionally consider that the National Oceanic and Atmospheric Administration estimates that 95% of the world's oceans remain unexplored and unseen by human eyes.

All of these big numbers and interesting percentages don't prove anything specifically. I do feel that it begins to show the situation in an objective scientific light. It reveals a huge possibility, if not probability in a quantitative perspective. Indeed, the most recent estimates by the International Ornithological Congress put the number of different bird species worldwide at 10,448. I further feel that this illumination of a fringe topic easily pushed aside by detractors using low brow emotion reveals the very real issue, very worthy of further research and investigation by scientists. Moreover, including the observational experiences of witnesses that can either be verified by other data or add new data sets to the pool of information on the subject will undoubtedly aid in revealing answers over the long term. What those answers are as of yet is open to speculation. In truth, we are still formulating the questions.

To revisit all these numbers another way, is there a case to be made if there are upwards of 98.2 million species yet to be identified on the planet and 95% of the world's unexplored oceans for them to currently call home? Shouldn't scientists by definition take an interest in such "monstrous" reports? Of course, to clarify, when some organizations cite numbers such as these they are speaking towards many new species that will likely be more different on a subtle singular characteristic, rather than larger overt ones such as horns that emit light. However, the potential remains for an eight-foot-tall winged creature to be discovered, especially in the world's oceans. Not that I'm one to seek out debate, or evangelise my view, but this is only one of several clear reasons why I find my adventures into the paranormal worthy of my limited resources.

These points, of course, leave out the most poignant area of paranormal study. The possibility of more supernatural explanations is an entire supplementary arena of variables to consider. Whether we are discussing the countless Bigfoot sightings occurring in conjunction with UFOs or otherworldly portals appearing and disappearing before witnesses' eyes, there are plenty of odd potentials to explore as sources for the Van Meter Visitor. As you may likely gather from my writing, my current personal favorite is exploring quantum physics and those theories attempting to explain multiple dimensions in order to make broader scientific theories unite. To clarify an important point in regards to our research and investigation into things such as the Van Meter Visitor, we should adjust our terminology. The issue is a small one of semantics. The scientifically inclined paranormal investigator is seeking as much quantifiable data as possible. This data can hopefully then, over a span of time, be used to reveal trends. These trends can be used to create profiles. These profiles of any particular phenomena can then become models. It is these models that scientists can then form into a testable theory due to a certain extent of predictability. This, of course, in the paranormal field is where things can get a bit mushy if not outlandishly difficult even with a healthy budget—which nearly never happens. Not to be taken lightly, these multiple dimension models are put forth by some of the most brilliant minds holding some of the brightest IQs today. There are several of these models and theories, such as M and String. These areas hold great chances to explain the possible sources of all things paranormal. Ultraterrestrial existence becomes a more palatable source for many of the more unusual reports that I go investigating, the more I get "out there." Adding more quality data to build a better ultraterrestrial model around may hold new answers to future generations.

8
Blatant Hoax or Practical Joker?
by Chad Lewis

Some skeptics will find this case so bizarre that they will blindly dismiss it as an elaborate hoax. In order to determine whether the entirety of events that took place in Van Meter was hoaxed, we must look at two core questions.

1   Who was the perpetrator?
2   What motive did the perpetrator have?

Let's start with question one, "Who was the perpetrator?" As fate would have it, the entirety of the mysterious happenings in Van Meter remains relatively unknown due to the fact that the town did not have an operating newspaper to completely cover the bizarre events of 1903. The lack of any daily, weekly, or even monthly newspaper/newsletter is in itself an oddity. Surely a town with a population of over 1,000 could have supported some form of printed news, yet residents of Van Meter had to rely on the nearby publications of the *Dallas County News* or the various Des Moines papers to keep abreast of the news. Eventually, Van Meter would get a newspaper called *The Reporter*, but exactly how long it was published is still unknown. By contrast, the 60,000 people of Des Moines, which sat a little over 20 miles to the east of Van Meter, enjoyed numerous daily and weekly papers in both English and German. In fact, a 1902 article in the *Des Moines Daily News* expressed the need for a weekly paper in Van Meter stating, "Some energetic printer with a little money could readily build up a fine business in Van Meter." Unfortunately, the lack of any local printed press meant that the only original source material we have is the article written by H.H. Phillips that was published in the *Des Moines Daily News* on October 4, 1903.

The Phillips article must have generated an enormous amount of unwanted attention for Van Meter, because in the days following two separate articles (perhaps by the same person) were published looking to debunk, or at the very least, minimize the weirdness of the original story. I will analyze each article separately, in the order that they were published.

First Article

Some citizens seemed upset by the newspaper attention

On October 5, one day after the Phillips article was published, the *Des Moines Daily News* (the same paper that printed the original story) printed the following article:

Van Meter Mystery Not Solved
But the report by Phillips was much exaggerated
Is it a robber or a joker?

Van Meter, Oct. – (Special) The "mystery" that has served to considerably excite the residents is still unsolved. The account sent to newspapers by H.H. Phillips was however, considerably exaggerated.

The fact is that instead of there being some prehistoric or antediluvian monster living in this vicinity, there is either some very active practical joker or some energetic robber at large.

It is true that divers persons have been disturbed by various sounds and lights and that one bank official fired through the front of the building in a vain effort to hit some object that had awakened him by throwing a bright light through the window.

Mr. Phillips has exercised his imagination to "build up" a stronger story for newspaper publication by weaving fictitious details with the genuine.

Upon reading this article several interesting points immediately stood out to me. The first thing that caught my eye was the fact that the article was a "special" to the newspaper, as was the original Phillips article. Being a special to the newspaper meant that the article was not written by journalist for the *Des Moines Daily News*. Articles that appeared in the newspaper were usually written by a freelance writer/journalist, yet it was not uncommon for ordinary members of the community to express their beliefs through a "special" article. The underlying fact that neither article was written by a journalist forces us to wonder what level of investigation went into each piece. Not knowing the identity of the follow up article's writer, and thereby not being able to address their character, simply adds another level of mystery to a case that is already engulfed in it. Another interesting aspect of the article lies in the admission that "various sounds and lights" had been reported by several (divers) people of Van Meter, be they paranormal or not. The author confirms that a bank employee (Mr. Dunn) had indeed fired his weapon at an unknown bright light, yet instead of the light originating from a hideous monster, the author claims it was nothing more than a brave robber or daring practical joker, neither of which were ever caught or even identified. The theory that the light was cast by a bold bank robber does seem plausible seeing that it was the bank building that was being visited. But then how do we account for the fact that Mr. Dunn fired point plank at the intruder with a powerful shotgun to seemingly no effect. The next morning, a search of the area resulted in zero evidence to support that the mysterious light was exactly caused by an intruder. Granted, 1900s crime scene investigation was pretty simplistic, but without a dead body being discovered, no trail of blood, and no other obvious signs of a robber, we have to assume that Mr. Dunn miraculously missed his target, or entertain the possibility that perhaps the light was cast by something much more devious than a two-bit robber.

The robber explanation is further diminished by the absence of any other reported thefts during the encounters. If a brave hearted soul was prowling around Van Meter at night, somebody forgot to tell him to steal things. Again, either this was the world's worst thief, or something else decided to visit Van Meter.

The idea that the creature could have been a hoaxer stretches credulity even further when weighed against the physical characteristics of the unknown creature. In 1903, people in the United States were smaller in both height and weight than we are today. In fact, at the time of the sighting, the average height of an American male was only five feet six inches. Meanwhile witnesses claimed that when the mysterious creature finally stood erect, it towered over eight feet tall. Of course, someone of average height could have been utilizing some type of stilts, spring or riser contraption. If that were the case, though, they would also need near super human agility in order to quickly descend telephone poles and dart from one rooftop to another as did the unknown visitor.

The article also postulates that the bright light was caused by some unknown practical joker who thought it would be hilarious to wander out at night to try to scare several well-armed residents. While this theory is certainly not impossible, evidenced by the countless practical jokers and hoaxers who have met their fate in the midst of their ruse, it just doesn't seem that plausible that the perpetrator would continue on with the prank for several more nights after having been blasted with gunfire by at least three separate people.

Another important clue comes from U.G. Griffith, who first noticed the strange light hovering over the town. Mr. Griffith reported that once he spotted the light above the Mather & Greggs building it quickly darted across the street and appeared on the top of another building before disappearing into the night. The description given certainly implies that the light maneuvered in a manner not resembling that of someone with a lantern or electric headlight. Barring that the robber moved at the speed of light, it seem improbable that any known human could have manipulated the light in the exact manner Mr. Griffith saw it.

Inside of Griffith Brothers Implement Store

Second Article

The second rebuttal was published on October 6, 1903, two days after the Phillips article, by the rival paper *Des Moines Daily Capitol*, with the headline:

Van Meter Hot Under the Collar
Town has been maligned by ghost stories
Citizens of the place feel indignant over the matter,
as it gives the place an unenviable reputation

The town of Van Meter is justly indignant over a series of articles that have appeared in the *Daily News* and the *Capitol* is in receipt of a number of letters from citizens of that place who feel highly indignant over the matter. The articles alleged that the town was highly wrought up over the alleged affair. The principal article started out with the following:

"Quite frequently one hears of a haunted house, but for a whole town to have 'em' is a different proposition. Van Meter, a town of about 900 souls, lying 20 miles west of Des Moines, alone enjoys the distinction of being haunted. Queer noises are heard, hideous apparitions are seen and uncanny lights move around in a mysterious manner."

In a letter received by the *Capital* it was stated, "It is very apparent on the face of every sane person that it is pure fabrication, but to the residents of the town here it is the height of foolishness. It seems as though the corporation manufactured this story from an incident or two and sent it into the news. They published the yarn and then began to investigate its source. They sent several telephone calls to the central office here asking concerning the party and stating that he was the author of their rampant story. That is generally their way of doing business."

"A traveling man with Swift & Co. of your city was in town today and came around to see the ruins, but there was none in sight." "Now we would like for you people to devote a little space to this attached article with the purpose in view of squaring us with the outside world and showing the policy of the *News* in first publishing such articles and then investigating the source."

Again, the author of this article alludes to an "incident or two" that actually happened, but these events were completely blown out of proportion by H.H. Phillips. Unfortunately, the specifics of these alleged events never came to light, and the reader is left to speculate on which aspects of the story were embellished and which parts truly did occur. Perhaps it was only the mysterious vanishing lights that were spotted, or maybe the creature sighted was only 5 feet tall rather than eight feet, but those important details are not known. Researching this case was reminiscent of trying to put together a puzzle that had huge chunks of pieces missing.

If the events that were said to have occurred in Van Meter were indeed hoaxes, then who was responsible for them? The most likely candidate is that of Mr. H.H. Phillips. As the author of the original article, he simply could have taken the real details of a botched bank robbery and let his imagination run wild in order to sell a story. One aspect of this reasoning that never quite sat right with me is this question: Why would someone in Phillips' respected position risk his career and credibility to push such an incredulous case? On a similar note, if someone was going to create such a hoax, it might not serve them well to implicate some of the town's most powerful and respected citizens in their ruse. If the event was a hoax, surely the men named and quoted in the article would have been furious over their attachment to the outlandish case. But all of this conjecture is based on the assumption that Phillips acted alone in perpetrating this hoax. We also have to explore the distinct possibility that all the people listed as witnesses might have been heavily involved in the trickery, too.

It is not unheard of for towns to look to the paranormal as a marketing tool that could put their town on the tourist map. The Rhinelander Hodag, The psychic Fox sisters, and the Fiji Mermaid are just a few examples of outright hoaxes that were meant to lure tourists in and part them from their money. On a weird coincidental note, one of the most infamous hoaxes of the 19th Century had its roots in Iowa. On October 16, 1869, workers digging on a farm in Cardiff, New York, "discovered" a 10-foot-tall prehistoric looking petrified man that was soon dubbed by newspapers around the country as the "Cardiff Giant." The hoax was orchestrated by entrepreneur George Hull, who traveled to Fort Dodge, Iowa, where he hired several laborers to carve out a giant 10-foot block of gypsum under the ruse that it was intended to be used for a monument for Abraham Lincoln. He then had the block carved into the form of a giant human and buried in Cardiff where it could be "found" at a later date. Not even Hull himself could have been prepared for the onslaught of media exposure and scientific inquiry that the giant generated. Ironically, it was the obscene amount of attention the giant received that would ultimately lead to its undoing and subsequent unmasking as a clever hoax. Because of the long line of financially successful hoaxes and frauds, out of all the theories of the Van Meter Visitor being a hoax, the idea of it being a tourist campaign holds the most weight with me.

The Cardiff Giant

But before we completely trash H.H. Phillips' name, we should at least explore the idea that he could have been an unknowing participant in someone else's elaborate hoax. It is also possible that H.H. Phillips was simply reporting events that he felt were accurate, when in actuality the events were nothing more than dime novel tales brewed up by unknown sources.

When all of the above possibilities are taken into account, one is left with more questions than answers. After looking at all the available evidence, we have no obvious reason to doubt the sincerity and trustworthiness of H.H. Phillips. We have even less of a reason to tarnish the exemplary reputations of everyone else that is tied to the case.

9
Possible UFO/Alien Connection
by Chad Lewis

If H.H. Phillips did indeed fabricate this entire fantastical story, his vivid imagination was decades ahead of any known UFO literature. Many of the circumstances that were reported in this case could easily qualify Phillips as a psychic, as he was able to foresee key components of alien abduction lore that would not surface for nearly 60 years. In fact, those with detailed knowledge of the study of UFOs (ufology) would be hard-pressed not to spot several main components of this case that squarely place it within the confines of a modern day UFO/alien encounter. Erratic bright lights maneuvering under seemingly intelligent control, strange beings that are all but bulletproof, and unidentified odors that leave witnesses baffled and confused are all hallmarks of UFO / alien abduction research.

1. Mysterious lights in the sky

When U.G. Griffith returned late at night to Van Meter and spotted a strange light hovering over the Mather & Greg building, his initial thought was that he had inadvertently stumbled onto a robbery in progress. However, his assumption must have quickly been squashed. As soon as he approached the unknown light, it quickly darted across the street to another building before finally disappearing into the night. In his article, Phillips claims that "little attention was paid" to Griffith's story, a fact that is very common in UFO sightings. Often times, witnesses who report seeing something unusual in the sky will frequently try to explain away the sighting, even if their explanation contradicts the evidence of what they just witnessed. It is infinitely easier to rationalize away an unexplained incident than it is to reconfigure human belief systems.

Mysterious lights in the sky would not have been that unusual to the Iowans of 1903—not an everyday event, but certainly not unheard of. Just a few years prior to the unknown light appearing in Van Meter, the state of Iowa, along with much of the rest of the nation, was in the middle of a rash of unknown airship sightings. In 1897, people all around Iowa reported seeing a strange ship-like object floating through the night sky. The *Waterloo Courier* extensively covered the event, claiming that "when first seen the mysterious object was at an angle of 35 or 40 degrees from the horizon and seemed to be almost twice the size of the largest and brightest star. In fact it did not look different from an immense star. With the naked eye it could be easily seen that the mysterious stranger was swaying from side to side." But what was once thought to be some sort of unidentified airship soon developed characteristics mirroring that of the Van Meter light. On April 7, the *Waterloo Courier* reported on several strange sightings out of Vinton, Iowa, where many prominent citizens "whose honestly is unimpeachable" bore witness to the unknown flying object that first appeared low in the sky. Around 9 p.m. the object "could be plainly observed to travel in a swaying manner like a bird, flying against the wind, darting to and fro, up and down, and was plainly visible for nearly half an hour." As the days passed, the sightings continued to getter weirder and weirder. The April 10 *Waterloo Courier* article carried the story of J.K. Joder, a west side druggist, who was heading home "about 1 o'clock this morning and when near the corner of Washington and West Forth Street was filled with wonder and awe on beholding what seemed to be a monstrous bat gliding through the air and coming toward him." He first described the object as "an immense black object with what seemed to be eyes of fire." Joder approached the object only to discover that it was operated by several small-statured, odd looking "foreigners" who were speaking in a language not known to him. The foreigners were busily engaged in some sort of repairs on the craft, and when finished they "were up and off." The sheer bizarreness of the story aside, it is interesting to note that upon first sighting the light, Joder believed that whatever it was, it resembled a "monstrous bat," much like that of the Van Meter creature.

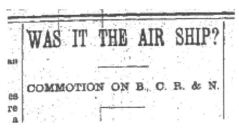

1897 Waterloo Courier newspaper story highlighting numerous Iowa sightings

On April 21, the *Waterloo Courier* continued covering the airship story, as the object was sighted in Waterloo, writing, "In the blackness of the night nothing could be discerned except two flickering white lights which moved side by side as they passed slowly over the west side, going northward." An interesting twist to the sightings was added when the *Courier* also covered the event as it happened in Iowa City writing:

> Many people here are confident that the airship of the later-day notoriety lies at the bottom of the Iowa River a short distance above the city. Shortly after dusk last evening several people were attracted by a meteorite like flash across the heavens and attended by a whirring noise that the passage of a heavy body through the air at a rapid rate might make. The light and the dark form which seemed to follow it approached the earth at a terrific speed and parties living near the river declare that it struck the water and immediately sank out of sight. Those who reached the point of the object's disappearance first claim that the water was churned into a whirlpool and that for a long distance the water was seething and boiling.

The people of Cedar Rapids also got in on the excitement, telling the *Courier*, "What we all suppose to be the airship has just passed overhead with three brilliant lights about 1,000 feet above us. One light is green, one red and one a bright white. It is going west and you may get a glimpse if it."

After hundreds of confirmed sightings, the people of Iowa were no closer to explaining the mysterious airship that was floating through their sky. Whatever this thing was, it was the talk of the state. Theories, speculations and cries of hoaxes were thrown around the saloons, dry goods stores and barber shops like hot moving town gossip. After covering many of the sightings, the *Waterloo Courier* finally weighed in on the mystery, opining, "Whether this is really an air ship, which some genius has constructed in some out of the way place, stored it with provisions for a long voyage and then suspending from it an immense beacon light and started out to amaze the people and keep them in a state of excitement; whether it is some heavenly body floating recklessly around in space or whether it is a visitor on its way from some of the other planets to the earth, can only be surmised. It's something, that is certain."

Mysterious lights in the sky continued on after the strange encounter of 1903. In July of 1907, the people of Des Moines were also visited by a strange light. The *Des Moines Daily News* reported that people in the area were very excited "about a strange light which bobbed about high up in the eastern sky last night." Although numerous theories were brought forward, no definitive explanation was ever given.

2. Impervious to human technology/weapons

If beings not of this earth posses the ability and knowhow to routinely visit and interact with us, it only seems logical that they would be in possession of technology which far outweighs our own. Trying to ascertain what capabilities this technology would have is something straight out of science fiction. Not knowing what "powers" these beings may or may not have forces us to proceed with caution when trying to sort out a plausible explanation. Based on the unusual events in Van Meter, we can safely assume that, whatever the creature was, guns appeared to have little or no effect on it. The first person in Van Meter to take aim at the beast was Dr. Alcott who "fired five shots at it at extremely close range, but either missed or the bullets took no effects." Undoubtedly coming face to face with a giant bat-like creature would understandably throw off Dr. Alcott's composure, and if this was an isolated occurrence I might be more open to the possibility that he simply missed the creature with all five of his close range shots. Yet amazingly, Alcott was not alone in his alleged poor shooting, because the very next night Peter Dunn would also discover that the creature seemed immune to gunfire. While bravely (or foolishly) protecting the bank's money, the mysterious light nearly blinded him as it blasted through the front window. With his shotgun loaded with buckshot, Dunn took aim and "fired point blank at the monster, tearing out the glass and part of the sash." Thinking that he must have killed the creature, Dunn waited for dawn to inspect the damages. Strangely, when morning finally arrived, Dunn was unable to find any indication that his shot actually hit something. There was no trace of blood, no bits and pieces of fur, feathers, or skin, and no dead or wounded body was found. If it wasn't for the shattered glass window, it might have seemed like his gun has misfired. Keep in mind that Dunn was using buckshot in his shotgun. Buckshot is a type of shotgun shell where several pellets of shot are placed in the shell and when the gun is discharged the pellets produce more of a scattergun effect, making targets much easier to hit.

Buckshot would have improved the chances of hitting the creature

The next person to witness the creature was O.V. White. According to the newspaper, he was normally a "good shot," yet he, too, failed to bring down the mysterious bat-like beast. A strange sound in the darkness prompted White over to his window, where, armed with his pistol, he stuck out his head and spotted the hideous beast perching fifteen feet away on a telephone pole. Waiting for his eyes to adjust to the darkness, White took "deliberate aim and fired," but instead of dropping the beast dead, his bullet seemed to only arouse the beast from its slumber. Showing no discernible signs of the gunshot, the beast flashed its light on White, emitted some sort of powerful odor (see missing time below) and then simply scampered down the telephone pole and flew off.

Having already survived three bullet-filled encounters with armed men, the beast would get one final test of its nine lives as a crowd of highly alert armed men gathered near the old coal mine waiting for the beast(s) to return. Town historians claim that when the beast returned it was greeted with a reception that could have "sunk the Spanish Fleet." Seemingly unfazed by the onslaught from the arsenal of weapons, the creature descended down the mine to the safety of its alleged hidden lair. So what kind of being could have survived so many shootouts with the locals? Could a prowler with primitive body armor (strong bullet-proof vests would not be produced until years later) have survived the onslaught? Odds are that even an extremely lucky prowler would have not been able to escape completely unharmed, which leaves us with the conclusion that whatever the being was, gunfire and bullets gave it no cause for alarm.

3. Missing time / False memories

On September 19, 1961, Betty and Barney Hill were driving along a rural stretch of New Hampshire road when a bright light in the sky caught Betty's attention. Something about the way the light was moving convinced Betty that she was not simply witnessing a falling star. Looking to capture a better view of the erratically moving light, the couple pulled over to the side of the road. Retrieving her binoculars, she was better able to see the multicolored lights as they danced around in the sky. Just as the couple was beginning to convince themselves that what they were witnessing was nothing more than a run-of-the-mill commercial airplane, the craft suddenly began descending towards them. A bit frightened, they hurriedly returned to the car and slowly began driving away while trying to keep an eye on the still approaching light. In a matter of minutes, the object was directly overhead, forcing Barney to halt their car in the middle of the road. Using his binoculars, Barney was able to see nearly a dozen humanoid figures aboard the craft. After hearing a series of odd mechanical buzzing and beeps, the Hills felt a bit numbed and made their way home with a feeling that something unnatural had happened to them. Noticing that they had fragmented memories of the weird trip home, the couple soon discovered that a normally four hour drive had taken them over seven hours to complete. The mystery of where the additional three hours of missing time went prompted the couple to undergo hypnosis, where it was discovered that the couple had been abducted against their will by the beings that were aboard the craft.

Betty and Barney Hill

The Barney and Betty Hill event was one of the first cases to popularize the idea of "Missing Time," which has become a staple in abduction research. The general idea is that those who are abducted often have trouble accounting for every hour of their time during their encounter. It is quite common for abductees to notice periods of missing time that can range from a few minutes to several days. Things get even more bizarre when abductees report having false memories implanted into their minds. One of the strangest cases of alleged false memories came from an alleged alien abduction case that I investigated in rural Bloomer, WI, where a woman reported numerous paranormal encounters that forced her to question her own memories. So many odd events had transpired in her life that the woman felt that some of her odd memories may not be actually what they seem. Here is an example of one of her encounters taken from my book, *The Wisconsin Road Guide to Mysterious Creatures*:

> Mary describes a truly baffling spotting of some unknown creature. Mary was working nights, and one evening when she left for work she spotted 'a very strange bird' in her driveway. She only caught a quick glimpse of the creature because it flew off so fast. Mary's description of the creature is as follows: 'It was white and about 3 feet tall or so, could've been 4 feet. It was not a crane because it had a bigger body and the neck was not long like a crane, and the head was bigger- not like a bird.' As Mary got into her vehicle and headed off to work the creature flew right in front of her, so close in fact that its feet hit her windshield. Mary stated, 'I thought I must have killed it and slowed down to look, but it just flew off.' It is interesting to note that later even Mary doubted the original 'bird' title she had given to the puzzling creature. Her description of some creature standing 3-4 feet tall with a small neck and large head is consistent with thousands of other abductees who often remember seeing similar shaped giant creatures that are often remembered as owls, squirrels, and deer, all of which match the same odd proportions that Mary described. Many of these "animals" turn out to be a type of alien dubbed "greys' that are very common in abduction lore.

I am still baffled by the question of whether, in an attempt to protect herself, Mary's mind was simply unable to recall the true nature of her encounter, or if some unknown force planted the false memory in her mind in order to prevent her from knowing the truth.

Of course, all of this information was useless to O.V. White as the mysterious creature hit him with a beam of light while releasing an unknown odor that would wipe the rest of the event from his conscious memory. Unfortunately, all we know about this mysterious odor is that it was able to "stupefy" him while preventing him from remembering any further details of the encounter. Basing our assumptions on the limited information makes it difficult to pinpoint the effect of the odor. Was the odor released on purpose, or was it a byproduct of the creature being shot at, much like a fearful skunk spraying its scent in order to ward off would be attackers? Perhaps it was the bright beam of light that caused Mr. White to part with his memory, which is constant with numerous other abduction cases. Oftentimes alien abductees have a hard time consciously recalling the entirety of their abduction. Bits, pieces and segments of the event are more often than not cloudy, scattered and fragmented, if remembered at all. The idea that White could not actively recall what happened to him fits perfectly in with established abduction lore.

With so many similarities between the Van Meter incident and what we now known about UFO/alien abduction research, it remains a legitimate possibility that what the people of Van Meter actually encountered was something not of this earth. Again, the binds of having such limited information on what really happened in this case assures that we are left with more questions than answers.

10
Misidentifications: An Examination
by Noah Voss

Misidentification seems to be a fact of life that happens to everyone at some point…whether you make the wrong turn on the road because you thought it looked like the right one, or maybe shouted someone's name in a crowded place only to have the person turn and reveal that they are not who you thought they were. Officers and lawyers must both be aware of this critical part of existence to accomplish their daily jobs effectively. A wide range of studies dating back into the 1800s have successfully documented the wrongful conviction of people for crimes they did not commit based upon witness testimony. For example, "The Innocence Project" has freed 239 prisoners after proving their innocence—including those awaiting the finality of their death sentence. Of those proven innocent under this project, 74% were wrongly convicted due to inaccurate eyewitness testimony. So it does happen. There is precedence for misidentifications from witnesses that mean well and are "together" enough to impress a jury of their peers at a trial. This, however, is a loose example for our most mysterious issue.

We are not discussing the finer details of human characteristics viewed at a distance, such as whether someone had a beard or a limp. Also, the human emotional state after witnessing a violent crime compared to that of witnessing something bewildering is markedly different. An example perhaps more akin to our witnesses in Van Meter may be that of catching a glimpse of a horse with odd shadows cast upon it and thinking, at least for just a moment, *"Wait…that looked like a zebra!"* before glancing back and seeing the whole situation clearer. This example, while perhaps a bit random, is understandable and probably frequent in nature. But when we are speaking about our 1903 case and possible misidentifications, it begins to strain credulity to think that our witnesses—often not expecting to see anything at all—report seeing a large, bat-winged creature standing taller than a man, with a horn on the forehead that projects a blinding light and is followed by a strong stench…all while still obtaining the ability of flight.

Establishing the Reality

Any intrepid investigator of the inexplicable will inevitably amass a huge number of witness interviews. But one cannot exactly go to school for this area of fringe research. In this section, I would like to discuss what every good investigator should consider with each and every witness interview— misidentifications. Whether correct or not, let us presume here two generalities for the 1903 Visitor sightings. The first assumption is that there was indeed "something" physically in the area causing our witnesses to see and or experience…well, something. No delusions, no sleight of hand hoaxes, no gas-release fueled hallucinations…our witnesses were seeing and hearing something. Second is that the "something" is of scientifically established origins: no mythical thunderbirds, no pterodactyls left over from the Cretaceous Period. In other words, not anything fun—just plain old established creatures.

If we can make these two assumptions, then one clear question remains: what were the residents of Van Meter seeing?

How about some other animal? Seems like a logical enough line of reasoning to at least explore. Some of the most detailed reports, sighted in the most ideal conditions, include wings on the creature with some ability of flight. So then could it have been a simple misidentification of a bird? Let's look at the bird-like characteristics as reported in the witnesses' own words. In the early morning hours of September 30th, Dr. Alcott has a Wednesday like no other.

He describes "great bat-like wings" and the next night Peter Dunn, the Van Meter Bank cashier, reports "great three-toed tracks" left behind after his terrifying encounter with the Visitor. Approximately 24 hours later, O.V. White and Sidney Gregg watched the Visitor from perhaps a 15-foot distance. Sidney Gregg remarks on "its huge, featherless wings" flapping as the Visitor moved away "with great leaps, sometimes using its wings to assist it," and with "wings extended" it then "sailed away" from view. During this same sighting, Sidney Gregg estimated the Visitor's height to be that of "standing at least eight feet high" as it stood erect after descending the telephone pole. Later on Saturday morning October 3rd, J.L. Platt, Jr. watched two Visitors exit a mine shaft and sail away. After this sighting, a "crowd of men and guns" gathered at the mine entrance later that morning hopeful to dispatch the Visitors should they return. Both Visitors did and were watched and fired upon with no clear response by the crowd as they descended into mine.

That's a lot of information, but what does it all mean for the Van Meter Visitor? If we look at the descriptions from the firsthand eyewitnesses and take them basically at face value, there are some insightful extrapolations that we can garner. It is important that we establish a few criteria first. The majority of known modern day birds have wingspans larger than their body length. Additionally, most all of our following examples have the bird's body length relatively proportionate to their approximate standing height. Actually, in most of the proceeding examples the bird's body length is longer than the standing height. To oversimplify, the body of a bird is smaller than its wingspan. Also, a bird stands shorter than it its long. To be clear, these are complete generalities for our examples.

We'll explore the bird potentials by name in just a bit. First let's try a quick little mental exercise.

A Mental Exercise

During speaking engagements, I often aim to interact with my audiences in dynamic ways. Let me try briefly through the written word. What is the largest bird you can think of that can fly? Make it one that you've seen in person. Got your choice? Even if you can't think of the name, a mental picture will suffice…besides, I've always been better with faces than names. So, whatever this bird's name or image is, how big would you think the wingspan to be? I'll give you a moment—go ahead give it a try. Remember, wingspan being measured wing-tip to the opposite wing-tip, if the bird were to outstretch both wings at the same time. Obviously if you're reading this, you have a certain interest and may very well know the physical characteristics of several large birds of flight. Would you venture a guess as to how tall the bird stands? Ponder that for a moment while I join you in this mental exercise.

Growing up mostly in the Midwest, but being fortunate to travel extensively in and out of the country, the largest bird that I myself have seen with great regularity would likely be the Bald Eagle. If I played along with these questions I'm posing to you, I would honestly have to answer that the largest Bald Eagle I've ever seen would probably have a 5-foot to maybe 6-foot wingspan. I'd probably further estimate that the Bald Eagle, on average, might stand just shy of 3 feet tall. Now, of course, I've never captured one and measured, but I have been within a few yards of at least a few dozen Bald Eagles in my lifetime. I was surprised to learn that the largest specimens have measured an 8-foot wingspan. Now those were of the Alaskan region, and none of my close encounters happened in Alaska, though some close to it in Canada. Indeed, the Bald Eagle is often cited as the largest bird of prey in the United States. So if we looked at the lower 48 and into southern Canada, the average adult wingspan runs between 5.9 and 7.5 feet. The high end height numbers put the Bald Eagle's body length at 3'3" and the average standing height at approximately the same. Interestingly enough, the population of nesting Bald Eagles was on a steep decline by 1903. Soon after—and for at least seven decades—there was no documented nesting Bald Eagles in the entire state of Iowa. I found it interesting to look at my own impressions as an experienced wilderness person and budding independent scientist. My own extrapolations were actually a bit smaller than the potential size of Bald Eagles that I have witnessed in my own lifetime. This rough estimate was born of easily more than 100 different sightings, many within a few yards distance, not including several stuffed ones within inches. If we extrapolate this very rough example to those witnesses having only one experience with some large winged creature, then their initial estimates may also be on the smaller side. This, of course, depends on each witness's personality and life experiences, which are difficult for anyone to accurately account for. What size of wingspan did you come up with for your choice of birds? Maybe the bird you were thinking of is in the listing below. I've compiled a short catalogue that contains some of the largest birds that were known to have called Iowa home in 1903. Let's walk through their size and characteristics to see if any of them are likely candidates for being misidentified as the mysterious Van Meter Visitor.

Native Birds

The Golden Eagle (*Aquila chrysaetos*) does have a uniform dark plumage and, while less identifiable as the Bald Eagle in the Americas, it is slightly smaller than our national bird with wingspans of 7'7" and body lengths up to 3'3". The Great Blue Heron (*Ardea herodias*) grows up to a 6'5" wingspan and can stand a notable 4'5" tall. The elegant Trumpeter Swan (*Cygnus buccinator*) is found in Iowa with up to an 8'1" wingspan, however much larger examples have occasionally been documented around the world, though body lengths have not been documented larger than 5'4" long. How about storks of the old baby fables? Iowa likely had only one native stork at the time of the 1903 Visitor sightings, the Wood Stork (*Mycteria americana*). With sturdy wingspans of 5'9", I could see why they were chosen for the precious cargo while standing a proud 3'7" tall. The Sandhill Crane (*Grus canadensis*) is often cited as the misidentified source of the infamous Mothman sightings of Point Pleasant, West Virginia by those choosing to ignore a mountain of other observational data simply due to the red markings around the Crane's head. The Sandhill Crane does grow to impressive sizes standing 3'9" tall, with wingspans easily approaching 7'; it is no wonder the Sandhill Crane is closely related to its Oriental cousin, the Sarus Crane...often cited as the world's tallest flying bird. In fact, the tallest bird naturally found in the wild in North America is the Whooping Crane (*Grus americana*), towering up to 5' tall with an imposing 7'5" wingspan. The American White Pelican (*Pelecanus erythrorhynchos*) has had wingspans measuring up to 10', coming second in North America only to the size of the California Condor. The American White Pelican also holds the distinction of being the longest native North American bird and can boast a body length of 5'8"...though a considerable length of up to 15" is beak, which would bring down its standing height considerably. So what does this all mean for the Van Meter Visitor sightings?

Speaking specifically to size, firsthand eyewitness Sidney Gregg estimated the Visitor's height to be "standing at least eight feet high." Perhaps he can be forgiven for exaggerating the size or simply being mistaken by a quick fleeting look at the Visitor through a wooded area in poor light? A lot of emotion and only a few seconds do not make a good scenario for observing details in any situation. As with most people who follow the Bigfoot enigma, this seems to be a fairly unfortunate frequent characteristic of reported sightings (though certainly not all). A quick recap of our Van Meter Visitor sighting on the evening of October 1st shows that a well-respected resident viewed this creature for many moments from no more than likely 15 feet away. Sidney Gregg watched the Visitor "perched" on top of the telephone pole in a near motionless position at first. Then he was able to view the Visitor use its body to ease itself down to the ground below. Mr. Gregg continued to watch on as it stood erect once on the ground, then more as it moved away from him flapping wings in a leaping motion. His sighting continued as the creature sailed away, likely in the air. That is a long few moments, and Mr. Gregg was afforded an extremely unique opportunity to view the Visitor in so many different positions and motions—including relative motionless! Those that might try to discredit the person instead of analyzing the observational data would be remiss to note that Mr. Gregg was not the only witness of this exact same sighting. O.V. White had been the first one to the scene this evening and also reported not only seeing the visitor perched upon the telephone pole, but he went so far as to shoot at it with no effect other than to cause the Visitor to move, illuminate and release a solid stench. So using this size estimate, even if off by 1 or even 2 whole feet, would still not match the size of any standing bird known to naturally be found in 1903 Iowa. The tallest example that could have naturally been in Iowa, and indeed the tallest bird found in the United States, is the Whooping Crane at an impressive 5' tall. Perhaps Sidney Gregg was just really off on his size estimate? To be fair, it would have been a very confusing situation to encounter something so mysterious in the dark of night. If the creature was a Whooping Crane standing at the highest end of current documented sizes of 5', then Gregg would have overestimated the height by more than 50% of the actual size of the entire bird! To look at it another way, if Gregg were to be 15' from me and I stand at 6'4" tall, he would have estimated my height to be 9'4". To err is too human, but that is a fairly large error. In addition, if you have ever seen a Whooping Crane, they are all thin neck and even thinner legs. They are majestic birds that can inspire much to be sure, however the sheer terror that clearly gripped 1903 Van Meter is not a very likely effect.

Two Whooping Cranes stand in the thin grass

A Foot Print

Thankfully, we do have another data point to gleam more information from regarding a possible source for the Van Meter Visitor—a foot print. Unfortunately, in the case of Cranes, it doesn't completely rule anything out. Cranes have three forward facing, un-webbed toes. However, they also have a small toe off of the rear of their foot. The problem with this for our data is that the rear toe is not always revealed in Crane foot prints. The ground has to be soft enough for the bird to leave a print, but not so soft as to have the foot sink in, revealing the shorter rear toe in the print. Sadly, at the end of the day, this doesn't prove or disprove anything. Without studying the missing plaster cast of the print, we can't rule out that it wasn't left by a Whooping Crane. Though, as is often the case when observing multiple tracks of bird feet, this rear toe becomes evident in at least one or more of the foot prints. In Peter Dunn's experience, it is noted that there were multiple prints. We should at least make note that most all of the birds of prey listed as a possible source for the Visitor sightings would not leave a three-toed print due to their anisodactyly toe positioning. These anisodactyl birds' feet leave a distinguishable four-toe imprint and often claw marks worth mentioning in their foot print. What are the other variables, then, to consider with misidentifications of the Van Meter Visitor?

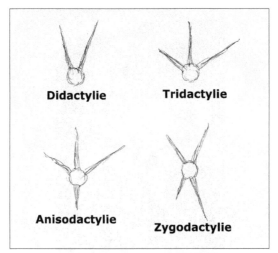

Bird foot biology as observed through tracks
(Created by Noah Voss)

The Dark Of Night

Well it was night, and we are admittedly not able to determine how lit up the area was— though by the end of the week, written accounts show that every light in town was left on all through the night. It may have also been raining, which would have likely made clear identification and size estimates additionally difficult. How about O.V. White? He did see the Visitor, and his reaction was so drastic as to raise his gun and fire. Indeed several witnesses shot at the Visitor—multiple times. Dr. Alcott was so offended by this mysterious creature visiting him that he fired all of his bullets save one. He was reported to have kept that final round as to have one last line of defense should this mysterious creature attack. Whether the final bullet was to be used on himself or the Visitor is lost to history. That is a fairly strong reaction to witnessing a Whooping Crane.

Birds of a Feather

So even if we take everything against our witnesses and just say they were several layers of wrong, we still have to deal with the observational data of the "featherless wings." Whooping Cranes have feathers and they need them to fly—I double checked. Indeed, all flight-capable birds lose that natural capability as soon as they lose their feathers. Parasitic skin diseases such as mange can cause molting or the loss of feathers in birds. If this were the case with the Visitor in Van Meter, I would put forward that it would likely make any feathers left on said bird much more obvious to the witnesses. Furthermore, if the Visitor was a natural bird within any stage of molting, it would still require the vast majority of the feathers on its wings in order to remain flight-capable. This sort of becomes a way for debunkers to explain away one observation, while at the same time making another observation completely impossible. For instance, one could say, "well the bird had molted, so that's why people reported bat-like wings." This isn't a valid explanation, however, due to the fact that multiple people then witnessed the Visitor fly only days after it was observed with the bat-like wings. This is not enough time for the feathers to grow back in. In fact, there are some species of birds that go through annual wing molts and lose the ability of flight for a time. However, even during these heavy molting periods, the wings of these birds do not have bare patches where skin would show through. So even if the Whooping Crane had some ailment or injury that caused its feathers to fall out, it would have remained sadly from the sky. Whatever was visiting Van Meter, multiple witnesses over multiple nights watched it fly.

We could discuss actinofibrils only recently found in fossil remains of Pterosaurs, revealing the complicated structures that their wings truly were. That would bring us to pycnofibres likely similar to the hair structure covering modern day bats, though not their wings. This, of course, would open up the antediluvian potential source for the Visitor sightings, which is a topic and discussion only covered in proper detail when it is the focus of entire books. I would like to at least mention that there are those in the Cryptozoological field that feel strongly about the possibility of extinct creatures still roaming the corners and caves (or mines) of the world. Indeed, there is precedence for these concepts such as the often cited Coelacanth. This large ocean dwelling fish was believed to have been extinct for 65 million years until found alive in 1938.

To play the other side of possibility, it is of course a potential that, due to the unique circumstances surrounding Sidney Gregg's sighting, he simply mistook the wings for featherless. Perhaps a dark-feathered, large bird witnessed in the night could be more understandable for missing the feathers such as a Turkey Vulture (*Cathartes aura*). I still remember my first Turkey Vulture encounter. I was on a classic back country road, both winding and full of hills, when all of a sudden this huge dark-plumaged bird hopped up from out of view and took flight. It was massive and startling, yet I could clearly discern what it was and that it had feathers and no horn, even though I was passing by in a speeding car. Admittedly, my sighting took place in the light of day. The Turkey Vulture can grow to have wingspans of 6' though their bodies have not been documented longer than 3'. Fortunately for the validity of Mr. Gregg's wing observations, we have another firsthand eyewitness—Dr. Alcott, who one day prior watched the Visitor and its "great bat-like wings" as the "half human and half beast" paid him a startling visit. It is also very unlikely that the climbing observations made by Sidney Gregg would be a Whooping Crane; even as tough as I'm sure they were in 1903, using their beak in the descending fashion of a "parrot" is not typical. So if we are still going to overlook all the observational data by our three eyewitnesses so far, and just assume that they got it wrong—not just wrong mind you, but very wrong…with size estimates off by 3 feet or more on something only 5 feet to begin with… somehow missing the feathers on an entire set of huge wings—then there is still the solitary matter of a single horn.

Horns

Our previously introduced witness, Dr. Alcott, remarked that the Visitor he watched in terror had "a blunt, horn-like protuberance" extending from the "middle of the animal's forehead." Again, if we looked at the known bird species as possible sources for this Visitor, we would have to look at the much, much smaller Cardinal, Blue Jay or slightly larger Wood Pecker that can have tufts of feathers standing near the top of their heads. To make that fit though, it would be a must for all of the other observational data to be forgotten or dismissed, something that seems even a bit much for someone who doesn't want to believe. Oddly enough, the American White Pelican grows an appendage off of the top of its beak during mating season each year. I'll admit that during my research for this case my heart sped for just a moment when I dug up this factoid. Mind you, I wasn't thinking "mystery solved." However, it complicated things. After all, we know that Pelicans were in Iowa in 1903, and as discussed earlier they can reach massive sizes in the bird world, even though smaller than the Whooping Cranes potential standing height. The growth on the White Pelican is often called the Pelican's horn or plate and looks less like a traditional horn than that of perhaps the fabled unicorn. The horn is laterally flattened down the length of the beak, and reminds me more of a dorsal fin on a fish than a horn.

White Pelican with "horn" growth visible on the top of the bill

Of course, we could look to some larger native bird and speculate that it had an extremely unique cutaneous horn (mutation that can cause hornlike growths) perhaps as the result of some burn or trauma. These small growths are known to happen in a variety of species, including humans. This potential solution for one characteristic brings the usual problem of still leaving too many other witness observations unexplained.

Dr. Alcott, in addition to the "horn," recounted the terrifying "bright light shining" during his sighting, stating that this "dazzling light…fairly blinding" him seemed to emanate from this horn. This is clearly an ability Pelicans are not known for. Indeed, the first sighting we have that may be connected to the Visitor is that of U.G. Griffith, who watched a light similar to that of "an electric searchlight" dance about the roof tops of Van Meter as it "sailed across to another building and disappeared." The Visitor and his accompanying "presence of a light of great intensity" were viewed by Van Meter resident Peter Dunn during his early morning sighting also. I feel like we've reached a tipping point in our potentials for misidentification.

Two Legs or Four

The native bird misidentification potential for the Van Meter Visitor source is getting slim to none. Those birds that could have been misidentified as the Visitor—displaying all of these characteristics or even most—simply do not exist. Just in case you still have your doubts, and good for you if you do, the Visitor was witnessed to have one more unique characteristic—running on all fours. Yup, don't see many birds running on four legs. Sure, we've watched the Road Runner put many a things over on old Wile E. Coyote, but always on two feet. After the Visitor descended the telephone pole, Sidney Gregg watched the Visitor as it "ran on all four feet, with wings extended, and sailed away." Through the documentation that we've dug up and from how it reads in the body of the original paper, my personal take away is not that the Visitor was using some sort of developed hand protruding off of a wing ridge. Bats have this in a way, but only in a developed claw that is technically the bats thumb and wouldn't be much use for running. Indeed, in the first article that we could find detailing these odd accounts, Mr. Gregg is said to describe the Visitor's movements on the ground "like a kangaroo, with great leaps, sometimes using its wings to assist it." Again that just doesn't feel like a bat to me. It does sound a bit like a large to very large bird, but we've begun to rule this out as a likely source too—even if just anecdotally through 100-year-old eyewitness accounts. But if we are to stick with the two criteria that I set in place in the beginning of this section, our witnesses did see something. So then, let us explore the bat potential.

Bats

This will be easy; there are no bats with single light-emitting horns anywhere in the world that we know of. In addition, the largest bat naturally found in Iowa would be best measured in inches rather than feet. The largest bats in the world are of the Pteropus species and have had documented wingspans of up to 5'7", however are biologically constructed to climb and fly more than walk, let alone run. These would not be natively found in Iowa either. Add to that, none have four clear independent legs. So, if not native birds or native bats, what else? We haven't discussed yet the night aspect to most all sightings of the Van Meter Visitor. What then do we know native to the Iowa area that might have nocturnal tendencies?

Owls

There certainly was a population of owls and even birds that have documented night prowess. Iowa is known to be home to more than a dozen species of owl. The Great Horned Owl (*Bubo virginianus*) calls Iowa home, and with the obvious "horned" in its name one might think we've got a potential source for the Visitor sightings. If you recall our eyewitness Dr. Alcott recounted quite clearly a "single blunt horn that grew out of its forehead." The Great Horned Owl garners its name from the two ear plumage points towards the top area of its head. Though named "horned," the owl's feathered ears are set far apart and would be difficult to mistake as a single blunt horn protruding from the forehead by most any observation. The Great Horned Owl is one of North America's largest owls but barely reaches a 4' wingspan and has a body length normally less than two feet. This is a far cry from the "standing at least eight feet high" estimate by Sidney Gregg…not to mention it doesn't address the running on all fours, the light or the presence of featherless wings. If an owl was not mistaken by the townsfolk as the mysterious Visitor, then was it perhaps some other nocturnal bird?

Non-Native Birds

It is possible that the Magnificent Frigatebird (*Fregata magnificens*) could have been passing through the Van Meter area? It does have a wingspan of up to 7' and some slight nocturnal habits. They are, however, known for having difficulty walking and taking off from flat surfaces. If one were to have been on a telephone pole, it would have been much more likely to launch itself from the perch rather than climb down to the flat ground. It would have also not likely used its beak to assist its climb. Of course, O.V. White was shooting at whatever it was he and Sidney Gregg saw on top of the telephone pole, so there is the added complication of a potential injury. The male of the Magnificent Frigatebird species does have very notable scarlet throat coloring that it is able to inflate like a bright balloon. Though not illuminated like a search light, this still would have been a distinct characteristic very likely mentioned by all of the witnesses—unless it was obscured somehow during some of the sightings. At the very least, it would stand to reason that this colored throat would have been observed by at least one of the many witnesses. If it was a female Magnificent Frigatebird the scarlet pouch would have been replaced by a distinctly white chest. This again would have likely been mentioned by at least one witness, though the glaring lack of any color given to the Van Meter Visitor by any of the witnesses does bring me frustration. Professionally this is not the first time that I have encountered this otherwise obvious characteristic being absent from eyewitness testimony. Saving you from my lengthy ramblings on the psychological and biological processes that may account for this, it is of my professional opinion, barring any new data, that the Visitor was likely of a uniformed dark neutral color. This personal belief would also go against the Visitor being many of the largest birds from the area—including the Whooping Crane and American White Pelican—that are often mostly white with varying patterns of colors. As we should discuss all gathered data likely connected to the Van Meter Visitor, we must examine the print discovered during the Peter Dunn sighting. The "great three-toed tracks" described could not be left by a normal, healthy American White Pelican due to the simple fact that they have four toes. Another fair point to bring up is if the print were of webbed feet, that substantial fact would have likely been reported in the original newspaper description. Admittedly this observation about the track documented by Dunn not being webbed is pure speculation on my part.

There are other birds with large wing spans in North America that could have uncharacteristically found their way to the Van Meter, Iowa region. Such luxurious hobbies like collecting exotic pets, while today have gained popularity, were not so in 1903. The number of zoos was also significantly smaller throughout the country in 1903.

Displacement of animals in nature has, however, been well documented. Normal causes range from displacements as the result of large forest fires to strong storm fronts, often hurricanes affecting entire regions, blowing animals hundreds of miles or more off course. The California Condor (*Gymnogyps californianus*) may be one of the closest and largest birds that could have unnaturally found its way into Van Meter. The California Condor often holds the distinction as having the widest wingspan of any land bird in North America. The environment in its natural habitat has evolved drastically over the last 100 years and is largely the cause of its drastic drop in population. The California Condor can be found gliding over the Western region of the United States on its up to 10-foot verified wingspan. Indeed, fossil records reveal that the California Condor at one time could have been found across the entirety of America. The Condor species as a whole often goes days without eating, however it can at times gorge itself on so much food that it cannot take flight again for a time. This would be one potential situation for the Van Meter Visitor who was witnessed fleeing a telephone pole, hopping away, flapping its wings in almost a kangaroo fashion, though eventually leaving the ground and sailing away. Of course, this does nothing to explain the running on all fours, the light, the horn or leaving behind a three-toed print due to the fact it has more than three toes. The Condor does have startling features on a featherless head and powerful leathery legs. While the California Condor has been known to use caves for nesting grounds, the likelihood of one or more using a mine with a ground level entrance is less likely. There were many residents that had unexplained occurrences at the mine, including one of the final sightings that reportedly had the Van Meter Visitor exiting the mine. Due to the large size and wingspan of the California Condor, it seeks out cliff side caves and any higher perches that allow for easy gliding from the nest. These are the opposite characteristics of the Van Meter mine. Then how about we look at birds that were even further away from their native habitats?

Not only are these birds not native to Iowa, but they would not likely be naturally found in North America. As slim as the chance is that these birds would have been in Iowa 1903, it fair to say that it may be more likely than looking to more obscure sources.

The Bustard (*Ardeotis*) family is a huge African bird capable of lifting its nearly 4-foot-tall frame into the air on its wide 9-foot wingspan; of course it has feathers, but no horn, no lights and wouldn't explain the stench. The ocean loving Wandering Albatross (*Diomedea exulans*) is by most accounts the largest wingspan bird living, but again needs feathers to do so, and of course has no horn, no light and no putrid scent. The Albatross has been verified with amazing wingspans of over 12 feet. The unverified wingspan reports of Albatross have been mind bogglingly large at 17'5". The African Horned Screamer (*Anhima cornuta*), on the other hand, is not as large but does have a unique "horn" structure that grows off the head. It is, however, not a good match for the Van Meter Visitor's horn description as it is very thin and indiscrete as well as doesn't match the Visitor descriptions for the light, stench or bat-like wings and stands nothing close to 8 feet high. The Hornbills (*Bucerotidae*) species of bird does have a very distinguishing characteristic—a large horn-like structure above its beak. The largest of the Hornbill species has been measured with a body over 4' in length, and with a 5' wingspan would be quite a sight to the folks of Iowa in 1903.

Hornbill Bird circa 1897, though not likely to have been in the Van Meter Iowa area

Of course, the species could not account for the bat-like wings, the light or the strong smell associated with several sightings of the Van Meter Visitor. In addition, Hornbills often have easily distinguished colorful patterns and are not anywhere near 8 feet tall. The Horned Guan (*Oreophasis derbianus*) is another large bird approximately the same size as the Iowa native Turkey. The noticeable difference with the Guan is the single horn protruding from the head above the beak. This would seem to be a great match, but again the Guan fails to meet nearly all of the other observations made by firsthand eyewitnesses in Van Meter. The Cassowary (*Casuarius*) bird has several interesting characteristics for our case. A large, flat shaped horn protrudes along the top of the head down to the beak. In addition, this bird can stand an impressive 6'6" tall on a great three toed foot. Though very distant from Iowa, they are normally found in tropical New Guinea. In addition, they are flightless birds that have very colorful patterning around the head.

There are, however, other flight-capable birds that could be found in Iowa and that enjoy the protection that night can afford such creatures.

Nocturnal and Crepuscular

The Yellow-crowned Night Heron (*Nyctanassa violacea*) is more of a medium size bird. The Van Meter Visitor, if a misidentified bird, would likely have needed to be a large to very large category of bird species due to all the large attributes associated with it from the eyewitnesses.

There are three remaining medium to large nocturnal or crepuscular (very active during dusk and twilight hours) native birds in Iowa during 1903 that we have not yet discussed. All three of these are Nightjar species and, even at their largest, are nowhere near large enough to be misconstrued as "standing at least eight feet high" nor do they hold other characteristics such as horns or odd plumage near the head. So then, not a bird, not a bat…but what then? If we have not identified a clear or fairly likely potential source for misidentification, then what have we learned?

Another Perspective

Perhaps I need to make clear what I have found while aiming to learn more about the unknown. It is often not the answers you reveal in the end that is substantial, but rather what you've been able to rule out. Then, and only then, as an objective independent scientist can you move forward with what remains. Sadly, often times what remains is much larger in breadth and scope than what was eliminated. So why then…what could possibly be the need to seek that which may be unattainable? Perhaps some unconscious need to prove to oneself that mysteries remain in an ever shrinking world is a motivation that I cannot deny, though it has never been of paramount importance in my waking mind. I do enjoy watching people learn… to expose them to new knowledge and different larger ideas than they had previously entertained. It is perhaps too easy this day and age to simply dismiss out of hand such strange reports as misidentifications of something mundane. To do so, however, is to accomplish nothing but a disservice to your fellow humans. To blindly believe someone wrong in their observations, something they themselves experienced with their eyes, ears and nose just as you believe the things you experience is a simplistic view of the world. To dismiss their experiences out of hand is to go further from the realm of logic than to openly consider just the possibility that something exists outside your knowledge base. This something could be so foreign that you had absolutely no idea it was even possible. To many people around the world, I imagine this possibility holds much fear.

More to the point of the Van Meter Visitor, what are we left with for possible sources of any potential misidentification? Let's review. Nothing matches up for a clear misidentification. That was pretty easy. Of course, you could push and prod, bend and bastardize several of the birds we just reviewed into being the source of one or all of the sightings. Hell, you could even say that each sighting was of a different bird! Though this may appear unlikely, in truth, by the end of the week, after much dialogue ripping through the town of some unknown monster lurking about in the night, it begins to be easier to believe that someone could have had a slight emotional response to an otherwise natural bird. However, in order to make any native Iowa bird fit as the misidentified source you'd have to do a lot of contorting of the facts. We've already discussed the issues with the height. You'd also have to believe that at least two of the witnesses were not only wrong, but had the exact opposite observation (as was the case when describing the wings as featherless) but explain how the Visitor was still seen flying by several more witnesses. Indeed, several more witnesses would need to be completely imagining their observations of a very bright light emanating from the Visitor or somehow not able to tell that it had a different source than that of a bird. If you were still trying to make the bird source fit, then you would have explain or maybe just discount the strong scent associated with the sightings by at least two eyewitnesses. Even if a native skunk was also startled by the sight of the Visitor, it is a fair assumption that most Iowa residents are firmly aware of skunk scent in 1903. On at least three separate occasions, the Van Meter Visitor was fired upon by eyewitnesses with their own, often-nearby and sometimes worn on-person, guns. Perhaps this is a prejudice or romantic view I hold, but it feels like most of these not-so-long removed frontier town folk would be decent shots. The closest shots fired at the Visitor were likely from only a few feet away, though undeniably this was through a closed window. The other known range of shots fired was 15 feet away, and O.V. White was said to have taken "deliberate aim" before he fired that shot. The newspaper even qualifies him as "ordinarily a good shot." Instead of watching the Visitor drop to the ground, it only seemed to "waken it up." The light from the Visitor and the odor that immediately followed the shot gives additionally accurate data about the light and odor that is even more difficult to explain away with natural or mundane sources. Even after these multiple gun-fueled attempts to rid the Visitor from Van Meter, it still flew. If one or more of the shots was true to aim, it would stand to reason that it may have not been able to fly if truly a normal terrestrial bird. Even if unlikely, it is still quite statistically possible that all the shots missed the Visitor, so clearly this point on its own is proof of nothing. That is the case with many of these observations by firsthand eyewitnesses. Each singular observational point that seems odd or difficult to associate with any other known native flying creature is not proof of anything. Nor are all of the ubiquitous unexplained observations, when all put together, proof of anything. They do, however, begin to reveal a problematic reality that remains a paradox to this day. That paradox is that very possibly there was something outside the realm of what the majority of people on Earth hold to know as truths.

We have discussed many birds. The problem with this as a comprehensive basis for the sightings is that none of them come close to clearly holding all of the characteristics described by the witnesses.

That is where we must leave it. The overarching potential that known animals were ever misidentified as the Van Meter Visitor is very thin. It just does not neatly fit, no matter how hard we tried. While misidentifications are still a potential, I hopefully explored to your satisfaction that this potential is not likely probable.

11
The Haunting of the Platt Brick Factory
by Chad Lewis

All that is left of Van Meter's mining and tile history is hidden on an old unassuming farm situated just a few blocks from downtown. It is hard to believe that one of the largest mining and tile operations in Iowa was situated on the land that is now sparsely grazed on by a few roaming horses. Unfortunately, the old mine shaft that seemed to function as the creatures' private entrance was shuttered and filled in decades ago, and mother earth provided the finishing touches of removing any remnants of an opening by covering the entire entrance with shifting earth. The mine shaft is so completely buried that it is impossible to pinpoint its location with the naked eye. The once proud tile buildings did not fare much better, as nearly all evidence of the tile plant's existence has been obliterated by time. Most of the old factory buildings were torn down long ago, their memoires recycled along with their brick foundations. The few remaining buildings are in such a state of dilapidation that their long term survival is all but impossible. The remaining bits and pieces of the old nearly forgotten tile factory may be decrepit, run down, and abandoned, but they are certainly not empty. Tales of brick throwing spirits inhabiting the structures have breathed new life into the story of the plant's history.

Even though the tile factory is located on private property, the strong lure of the haunted stories entices many visitors to venture out to the abandoned buildings in search of the phantom flying bricks. Once among the ruins of broken tile, visitors often hear the sound of bricks knocking against one another as though some unseen force was throwing them into a pile. Thinking that someone else must be out there tossing bricks, witnesses scour the area only to find that they are completely alone. Others have been startled when the quiet peacefulness of the area is shattered by the phantom sounds of old machinery rattling away exactly as it would have back in the early 1900s. These odd accounts of paranormal activity began spreading all throughout the region, prompting more and more people to make the journey to Van Meter.

Kevin Lee Nelson in front of remaining tile building

Just like in a gritty horror movie, most people choose to visit the old haunted location in the dead of night. On many occasions visitors have heard God awful screeching and screams coming from the abandoned factory. The fact that these nocturnal screams do not sound human causes further puzzlement from those who have been privy to them. There is some disagreement among witnesses as to whom or what to attribute the phantom wailing. Some folks claim that the screeching is that of the 1903 beast(s), believed by many people to be still residing in their old stomping grounds. Others firmly believe the horrific screams are those of formers miners and tile workers who died within the confines of the old plants. Regardless of which version is true (if either), these spectral bellows tend to cast a cloud of eeriness over the entire area.

Not surprisingly, the internet is flooded with ghastly tales of people having personal experiences with the paranormal, and the Van Meter brickyard is no exception. The website www.strangeusa.com posted several accounts from previous brickyard visitors. One posting tells of mysterious lights that have been seen roaming the area of the abandoned coal mine, although since no further specifics are offered, it is difficult compare the recent lights to the one given off by the original creature. Another posting from

January 2008 tells of a more sinister occurrence that befell a group of friends who wandered out to the brickyard only to discover several members of their group had mysterious bruises and burn-like marks after feeling as though something unseen in the darkness grabbed at them. In the summer of 2010, another visitor reported seeing the ghostly image of a person intently staring at them through a broken out window. Even though these alleged events are posted anonymously and not exposed to any type of examination or fact checking, they are nonetheless interesting and provide an ongoing cataloging of strange happenings on the land. It is still undetermined whether or not these encounters (which would be classified as ghost phenomena) are correlated with the monster sightings of 1903.

One aspect of the paranormal that has always fascinated me is the study of the development and progression that all legends inevitably take. It's much like the kids' game "telephone," where the story changes slightly as it is whispered from one person to another. I have discovered that many times specific information—the names of witnesses, the date of the experience or even the location where the experience took place—are often deemed interchangeable by the teller of such tales, even though the core of each legend remains unexpectedly stable. Each generation looks to configure, update, and twist the legend to fit neatly into its current understanding and reasoning. It is quite fitting that the haunted legend surrounding the tile factory entices visitors to the exact same spot where the hideous monster was sighted back in 1903. Does the land itself hold supernatural significance as though it were a supernatural beacon luring in susceptible believers, or have we as a society finally traded in our ancestral fear of deadly unknown creatures lurking in the dark and replaced it with a more modern fear of ghosts and spirits? Much like an art dealer looking to establish the provenance of a rogue painting, the sheer difficulty of tracking, following, and documenting these changes leaves gaping holes in our knowledge of these legends.

The location of the old factories may also play a significant role in all of the weirdness that takes place. Paranormal lore is saturated with unexplained events happening on, near, or around places that have been all but abandoned by society. Whether it is Mothman creatures prowling old bomb bunkers, or hellhounds inhabiting nearly forgotten rural train tunnels, it seems that supernatural beings prefer to set up shop in dark, dingy places where dust piles outnumber curious visitors.

After the tile and brick factory shut down for good, the land and remaining buildings were sold off to the X family (name withheld). During our first visit to Van Meter we had one simple goal—to find out who owned the old mine and get permission to check out the property. Now this may sound easy, but cold calling someone to ask if you can scour their land in search of a 100-year-old giant eight foot bat takes a bit of finesse. To help our cause, we turned to Jolena Welker (Van Meter librarian) many times when investigating locations in rural areas…having a local vouch for you is an indispensible ice breaker. Jolena called up the X family and informed them of our intentions. Within a matter of minutes, we had secured a personal tour of the old tile and mine grounds. At the gates of the old factory we met up with Mr. X, who was accompanied by his son and grandson who probably jumped at the opportunity to tag along and catch a glimpse of the weird people who were out looking for giant bats.

Chad Lewis at site of old mine opening

From the moment we met him, it was clear that Mr. X was a hard working, no nonsense type of guy. He looked like a stereotypical farmer straight out of a Hollywood movie—the type that seems to have nerves of steel that can handle any situation that life throws his way. After quick introductions, Mr. X began the makeshift tour. As were we strolling through the picturesque countryside surrounding the old mine, we stopped at the site of the original shaft opening where he began sharing his family's history on the land. Much to our surprise, his tough looking exterior softened a bit as he recalled the many days of his childhood spent playing near the old mine. Choosing his words carefully, Mr. X told us that although he had no good reason to fear the site of the former mine, the area had always given him the impression that something was not quite right. Needless to say, we were a bit taken back by this confession; Mr. X did not seem like one to fret over such things. The idea that the section of land where the mine once operated was somehow unexplainably different from the rest of the farm was echoed by one of his sons, who also expressed his trepidation concerning the old patch of land. It was a perfect sunny August afternoon, yet hearing of their uneasiness suddenly gave the area a much grimmer appearance as we slowly wound our way back to the main road.

From the beginning, we had assumed that the X family had tolerated our bizarre tour request only as a favor to Jolena, yet once we said our thank yous and goodbyes we were also granted permission to venture back during the night in order to stake out the old mine. We had already spent several nights wandering the old downtown during the wee hours of the night hoping that the Visitor would continue its habit of appearing at 1am. The middle of the night can cast an eerie quiet on the small downtown of Van Meter. It didn't take much imagination in order for our minds to conjure up the feel of autumn 1903. Strolling through the all but abandoned streets, we got a sense of what the witnesses must have felt when the uninvited creature descended upon their peaceful little town. It was amazing to tour the exact same locations where the creature had been spotted, and it felt as though at any moment someone might poke their head out of an overhead apartment yelling about a monster. The main difference between our nights wandering downtown and those of 1903 was that we felt that technology was on our side. Armed with a boatload of equipment, we felt that our cameras, audio recorders, motion detectors, night vision video, Geiger counters, EMF Meters and thermoscans would be far more effective in capturing evidence of the Visitor than the useless guns and knives that had failed the previous residents. Unfortunately, fate did not deliver the opportunity to test our equipment theory; the creature was nowhere to be seen. Thinking back on it, we were probably filled with the same superiority hubris that accompanied the witnesses of 1903, who also probably believed that their "modern" firepower was enough to overtake anything foolish to show itself in town. While investigating the town was one thing, spending the night near the old mine shaft opened up a whole new set of possibilities.

After several hours spent arguing, debating and bantering over what we believed would be the creature's supposed schedule, habits and behaviors, we decided to arrive out at the old mine around 11pm. Our plan was to stake out the old mine during the hours prior to when it was sighted in town, with the belief that it would have left its lair prior to it sighting. Unfortunately, the story of 1903 was never completed and we are left wondering how the townsfolk managed to close off the old mine shaft. It was our hope that perhaps the creature(s) had found another entrance/exit to the mine and was continuing to make nightly expeditions into the surrounding area…and we were hell bent on locating it. The crisp night air was overflowing with our excitement and anticipation around the possibility of spotting the beast exiting its former lair. Every so often the noise of the farm horses rustling would break the peacefulness of the night. By 1:30am the only moving creature we had seen was a stealthily moving fox that scurried past us. With little evidence of the creature, we walked back into town to see if the beast was making its nightly rounds there. After sweeping through the various creature sighting hotspots, we wanted to make it back out to the mine before the sun came up just in case we could catch the beast on its return flight. Although nothing supernatural appeared that evening, it allowed us to follow in the footsteps of the brave 1903 Van Meter residents who also spent their nights waiting for the creature to appear. Since our initial visit to Van Meter we have spend several more evenings in the darkness of night keeping a close and watchful eye on both the town and the old mine.

I was discussing this case with a group of my friends (who are not researchers) when they pointed out that perhaps I was just reading too much into the significance the land plays in the weird occurrences. Perhaps the haunted legend is not actually intertwined with the monster at all, and the fact that they both occur on the same area of land is nothing more than a mere coincidence. Analogous to the chicken and the egg question, does a place's reputation cause the legend, or is the legend responsible for the reputation? Perhaps we may never know.

12
Mass Hysteria
by Chad Lewis

On the morning of August 31, 1944, a bizarre series of gas-induced events began that would forever ensure the small town of Mattoon, Illinois a place in the annals of unexplained events. It began as a local couple nauseously awoke to the overwhelming odor from some type of unknown gas. The very next night another family was plagued by a similar vomit-inducing chemical, but this time an eyewitness spotted a tall man dressed in black lurking outside, near the family's open window. Over the next few days, more reports of this phantom anesthetist spread throughout the city as more and more people reported being sickened. Before long, the whole town erupted into an utter state of panic over this late-night prowling gasman, and within days the phantom man was being frequently reported throughout the entire city. To make matters more puzzling, the perpetrator possessed an uncanny knack at evading both the authorities and the hyper-vigilant townsfolk. On September 14, after dozens of alleged attacks, the mysterious gassing abruptly ended. With no culprit in police custody, theories put forth among the citizens ran rampant. Each one was more bizarre than the next, concluding with the idea that a half-ape, half-man was running through town with a spray gun filled with toxic chemicals. The case was never officially solved, a detail that acted like shark chum in attracting both skeptics and psychologists, who quickly pronounced the events as a classic case of mass hysteria. The weird events of Mattoon have gone on to become one of the most cited cases of paranormal related mass hysteria. Most people don't even pause to consider the fact that Scott Maruna, author of the most definitive book on the Mattoon events, *The Mad Gasser of Mattoon: Dispelling the Hysteria*, came to the conclusion that the mad gasser was a flesh-in-blood human being, albeit a slightly demented one.

That "Mad Gasser" Case Gets Scientific Analysis

The miasmic madman of Mattoon duced by a gas which was sprayed on
who had this hustling central Illi. the victims by some inamolaus fiand

Investigation into the Mad Gasser

While most experts agree that mass hysteria is indeed a real psychological ailment, many are far too comfortable in throwing the explanation out as a blanket answer for anything that stands out as being unusual. Because of the apparent similarities on how the Mattoon and Van Meter stories began, quickly progressed, and ended in mystery, the idea that Van Meter was nothing more than another case of mass hysteria does bear some consideration. I suppose it is possible that events which started with a simple light in the sky could, within days, blossom into a giant eight-foot bat that flies around the town with a built-in light while spewing out a mysterious memory-erasing odor.

There are several aspects of these events that I believe concretely knock away the label of mass hysteria from the Van Meter case. One of the main hallmarks of mass hysteria involves a sudden onset of irrational thinking and/or behavior accompanied by inexplicable symptoms of illness (like getting sick from a phantom gasser). But outside of O.V. White's sudden inability to recall key elements of his night, no other physical or psychological symptoms were reported by any of the witnesses, making the possibility that the events in Van Meter were nothing more than mass hysteria highly improbable.

There is also the inclusion of physical evidence in the form of the plaster casts that were allegedly taken of the mysterious three-toed beast. While the mind can easily conjure up hallucinations, misidentifications, and complete common sense destroying panic, being able to mentally manifest actual footprints is a bit more farfetched. That is not to say that the witnesses, after believing that they had just encountered something supernatural, could easily "see" what they wanted to in a normal set of footprints, much like seeing shapes and figures in clouds. To find evidence of this wishful thinking happening, all one needs to do is look at the thousands of "ghost" photos online where every strange shadow of light or twisted tree branch is suddenly construed as the outline of a vengeful spirit. Perhaps Mr. Dunn felt a bit foolish by his actions and used the footprints to help justify why he shot out the front window of the bank. But until more information on the event surfaces or someone discovers a strange set of plaster cast footprints in their attic, we may never know the real truth behind what happened in 1903. I think it is safe to say, however, that mass hysteria was not the culprit.

13
The Ultraterrestrial Theory: Tricksters, Daimons, and Quantum Consciousness
by Kevin Lee Nelson

The Ultraterrestrial Hypothesis

After researching countless cases involving allegedly paranormal (or simply unexplained) events, one will invariably begin to notice they share a number of common characteristics. It may be surprising to learn that seemingly diverse occurrences, such as UFO encounters, Bigfoot sightings, or run-ins with phantoms may all display shared traits and similar factors governing their appearances. In fact, it is possible that each of these bizarre events is actually a different manifestation or expression of a single root phenomena or intelligence. This theory has come to be known the "Ultraterrestrial Hypothesis."

The late John A. Keel first coined the term "ultraterrestrial" in his landmark book, *The Mothman Prophesies,* published in 1975. I should note that throughout this chapter I will frequently highlight events from the Mothman case, as I feel they parallel many of the mysterious events that occurred in Van Meter. Keel believed many anomalous events couldn't be explained by the standard extraterrestrial theory, which assumes beings from other planets, while strange, would still be subject to the natural laws of physics. However, this does not appear to be the case. According to many eyewitness reports they are not limited by physics as we understand them. Their craft have an ephemeral quality totally unlike earthly machines and are able to change shape, merge into one another and instantly disappear. They are not constrained by gravitational restrictions, are usually completely silent, and have been known to pass through solid matter. The bodies of ultraterrestrials can change shape and take on the aspect of creatures from myths and legends, or bogeymen that often reflect society's anxieties. Their behavior is equally strange and incomprehensible. A great number of incidents seem so bizarre and nonsensical that they appear to be the work of some kind of cosmic trickster rather than the handiwork of a presumably advanced race and rational civilization. This is one of the reasons ultraterrestrial events are so perplexing and difficult to study, as their origin, corporeality, and motivations cannot be determined. They are a total mystery. Do they come from a different dimension or time? Or do they come from within the deepest recesses of our own psyche?

John Keel also noticed that contemporary UFO and paranormal phenomena had a striking number of similarities to traditional European folklore, such as the appearance and behavior of elves and fairies. For example, he felt events surrounding alien abduction reports sounded remarkably similar to folk legends involving ill-fated people who are snatched away after trespassing into a "fairy ring," or mound deemed sacred to woodland spirits, never to be seen again. Legends also mention how unwary travelers could be struck by "elf shot," a sort of magical projectile or beam that paralyzes, sickens, or strikes the victim dumb. All are also common symptoms following alleged alien contact.

After countless incredibly bizarre personal encounters (all well documented in *The Mothman Prophecies*), Keel wondered if perhaps many unexplained events, which have gone on for centuries, are really one and the same, that is, different names for the same phenomena. For example, a person in the sixteenth century would naturally attribute odd phenomena, like strange lights hovering above a forest, to fairies. However, contemporary witnesses to a similar event would tend to view them through their own cultural context and interpret it as a UFO. What were once the "Chariots of the Gods" are now advanced spacecraft. But the real question is this: Are the entities' actions and appearance determined by the culture of the witnesses and the time in which they live—one man's "little green men" is another's leprechaun—or do these entities *intentionally* take on specific shapes as a form of guising to communicate symbolically through emotionally charged images and archetypes from our myths and legends?

Keel felt that ultraterrestrials are not aliens from distant planets, nor are they necessarily flesh-and-blood beings of this world. Instead, he was more inclined to believe they are *trans-dimensional* (or what some may call *hyper*-dimensional) entities inhabiting a plane of existence completely beyond our understanding...one that occasionally, or at certain unique places, intersects with ours. He noted:

> I have adopted the concept of ultraterrestrials – beings and forces which coexist with us but are on another time

frame; that is, they operate outside the limits of our space-time continuum yet have the ability to cross over into our reality. This is not a place ... but is a state of energy.

The Holographic Universe

Absurd and illogical characteristics common among UFOs sightings and extraterrestrial visitations is also explored by philosopher and visionary Michael Talbot in his book *The Holographic Universe* (1992). Like Keel, Talbot feels the extraterrestrial explanation is a woefully inadequate one which does not account for all (or even most) of the events surrounding extraterrestrial reports. For example, why are presumably highly advanced races bothering to engage in bewildering games with witnesses? Too many alien visitors are reported appearing humanoid with no problems breathing our atmosphere and seem too well adapted to our planet's gravity. Instead of appearing in major cities and presenting themselves to the leaders of nations they appear in small towns and rural areas making their presence known to farmers, housewives, and motorists on country lanes. Talbot is convinced we are dealing with something far stranger than our common conception of interplanetary visitors, stating:

> UFOs do not even behave as physical objects to. They have been watched on radar screens to make instant ninety-degree-angle turns while traveling at enormous speeds – an antic that would rip a physical object apart. They can change size, instantly vanish into nothingness, appear out of nowhere, change color, and even change shape (traits that are also displayed by their occupants).

He continues to describe UFO cases in which alleged aliens engage in bizarre behavior like singing goofy songs or throwing potatoes at people, even hallucinatory examples in which, "humanoid aliens shapeshift into birds, giant insects, and other phantasmagoric creatures." Like Keel, Talbot believes people have witnessed this type of phenomenon for a very long time. Naturally, each encounter was colored by the cultural understanding of the age in which the person lived, that is, the phenomenon is filtered, decoded, or broken down into recognizable concepts, symbols, and metaphors. Talbot writes, "When stripped to their underlying archetypes, all such phenomena are part of the same, vast, pulsating something, a something that changes its appearance to suit the culture and time period in which it manifests, but that has been with the human race for a long, long, time."

These are not mere hallucinations. Scores of cases include physical evidence after having contact with unknown entities including crop circles, burn marks, mysterious scars, or strangely incongruous objects left behind—even alien-prepared *pancakes* in one case in Wisconsin.

What is their purpose? Some, like crops circles, appear to be mysterious symbols containing a kind of hidden geometric meaning. In other cases people are left with nightmares and cruel physical reminders of bodily invasion, like alleged alien implants. Sudden and inexplicable appearance of random objects known as "apports" (from the French word "apporter" meaning "to bring"), is well known within the paranormal field and among Spiritualists. For example, coins, stones, or items lost decades ago, may suddenly appear on a table. These relics exhibit a very arbitrary and nonsensical quality, like residual figments from a dream. Perhaps the division between the physical and psychological worlds (or waking world and dream world) is not as great as we have come to believe, allowing objects and *beings* to move freely between states. In the case of the Van Meter Visitor, it was reported that physical evidence was left behind in the form of a large three-toed footprint. A cast was reportedly made of the print. Unfortunately, the whereabouts of the cast, or whether it even survived the last century remains unknown.

Reality Hacking

Keel and Talbot are not alone in their observations. Long before both of them, renowned UFO researcher Jauques Vallee proposed a very similar concept in his highly influential book, *Passport to Magonia: From Folklore to Flying Saucers* in 1969. Vallee was one of the first to make the connection between traditional myths and modern UFO sightings, stating:

> We are dealing with a yet unrecognized level of consciousness, independent of man but closely linked to the earth…I do not believe anymore that UFOs are simply spacecraft of some race of extraterrestrial visitors. This notion is too simplistic to explain their appearance, the frequency of their manifestations throughout

recorded history, and the structure of the information exchanged with them during contact.

Like Keel and Talbot, he believes the entities do not originate from somewhere in outer space, or an actual fairy realm, or the bottom of Loch Ness. Vallee feels the entities come from another dimensions beyond space and time, a multiverse in which our reality is only a single plane of a much larger whole, like a single facet of an infinitely-sided jewel. To take the jewel analogy further, perhaps consciousness is like light and is thus able to pass through multiple facets of reality at once. This idea corresponds with Talbot's "Holographic Universe" theory, as holograms are created by carrying information via light. When it passes through a decoding medium, like a crystal, a hologram is formed.

What makes Vallee's theory slightly different from the Keel's ultraterrestrial theory is his "Control System Hypothesis." Vallee's believes the unknown visitors seem to have a distinct purpose and agenda. He feels they have been subtlety influencing the development of our species for millennia and ever so delicately directing and influencing the course of our history like sinister puppet masters. For what purpose or to what end is anyone's guess.

In Talbot's "holographic" model of the universe, he believes what people are experiencing is neither a subjective nor an objective experience, but rather *both*...what he calls an "omnijective" experience—an event that is paradoxically both real and unreal. This is in some ways similar to French philosopher Henry Corbin's concept of the "imaginal realm," or *mundus imaginalis*, a territory that exists between the physical world of the senses and the spirit world. This is not an actual place, but rather a state of mind that is no less real than what we perceive to be the physical world.

But how can something be simultaneously both real and unreal? If you consider that everything we experience through our five senses are only interpretations, symbols, or metaphors applied to vibrating particles it begins to make a bit more sense. For example, what we may perceive as a "chair" is actually only a collection vibrating particles of varying density. There's something there, but it's not necessarily what you assume it is in an absolute sense. Through biological evolution we've developed sensory organs enabling us to make sense of our nebulous surroundings. We've created an order out of the chaos of vibrating particles, perhaps one subjective to our species, which has helped us survive. In addition, we've learned through our culture to perceive objects within a particular context. For example, when we notice a particular configuration of vibrating particles contains certain learned attributes, like four legs and a seat, it conveys a sense of "chairness" to our senses. However, the concept of "chair" is a learned form of comprehension. It is not innate. A caveman may look at the same thing and not see a chair at all; he may only see an odd configuration of firewood. It's up to our brains to translate what we are experiencing in the world around us, and occasionally those translations get garbled, especially if something has no context, like an ultraterrestrial.

To go one step further, when we begin to entertain the idea of non-localized consciousness interconnected through a quantum field, as many physicists do, the mystery only deepens. So is ultraterrestrial phenomenon real or is it all in our heads? The answer to that is, I believe, best summed up by author and mystic Lon Milo Duquette when he says, "It's all in your head … You just have no idea how big your head is." In essence, *everything* is consciousness. This hypothesis is by no means new. Noted psychologist Carl Jung believed that UFOs, usually referred to as "flying saucers" in his day, were the product of human collective consciousness.

What Keel, Talbot, Vallee, Harpur, and others are all saying is that our world—even reality itself—may be a lot stranger and far more plastic than we ever imagined, at least to the Western mind; some schools of Eastern thought and many so-called primitive cultures have accepted this idea for millennia. Could it be that all it takes is collective will or consensus acceptance of the reality of an idea or phenomenon to make it a physical reality? There are cases where scientists have discovered and observed new subatomic particles almost simultaneously, even though they were half a world apart conducting separate independent research. It was as if when one researcher observed the particle it mysteriously blinked into existence and became a reality in the other lab at precisely the same time.

One of the tenets of quantum mechanics is that observation or attention changes and solidifies realty. Our observation can actually affect the behavior of quanta (subatomic particles). This is known as "Heisenberg's Uncertainty Principle." In essence, for something to be "real" it must first be observed; as in the classic Schrödinger's Cat example, it takes an observer to create the reality that the cat is either dead or alive, a term referred to as "quantum superposition." Without the observer, the cat exists in a kind of limbo, neither dead nor alive (except to the cat of course!). In short, without an observer, reality remains in quantum superposition, nothing more than potential. Only when it is observed does it crystallize into physical reality and gain location. One could do further down this rabbit hole by referencing other related theories like "String Theory," its cousin "M-Theory," or further plumb the concept of non-locality, but that is far beyond the scope of this book.

Could it be that we are collectively and continually creating (or rewriting) the world around us through our own observations, desires, and will? It appears possible. Infamous British occultist Aleister Crowley defined magic as "The Science and Art of causing change to occur in conformity with the Will." If this is the case, are we continually engaging in magical creation through observation of our world? Could we be subtly, or unconsciously, directing trajectories of events whereby we become the authors and artists of our own reality? It's an interesting thought.

Allow me to give you a contemporary example: Sightings of Bigfoot, or Sasquatch, have exploded in recent years. There is even a TV show dedicated to seeking out and "Finding Bigfoot," as the show is titled. The very idea of the existence of a large undiscovered hominid was considered laughable just a few decades ago. Yet today some scientists are spending tremendous amounts of time and resources testing the hypothesis, some even claiming to have isolated Bigfoot DNA. Ever so slowly, an increasing number of people open their minds to the possibility of its existence.

Still, the Bigfoot hypothesis extremely problematic when one approaches it from a purely physical standpoint…that is, believing Bigfoot is a flesh-and-blood creature, a surviving relic of an as-yet undiscovered species of hominid. However, the Achilles heel of this theory can be summed up with one word: food. A creature that size (usually over 7 ft tall) would require an enormous amount of food, yet Bigfoot is repeatedly spotted in regions with relatively few sources of food, especially in winter. I have heard theories about the possibility of Bigfoot creatures stealing food from farms and orchards, but this doesn't hold water; vanishing crops of that magnitude would certainly be noticed. A full grown mountain gorilla can eat up to fifty pounds of vegetation in a single day; imagine the amount of food something the size of Bigfoot would require. Most environments simply couldn't support it, even in small numbers. Cryptozoolgist Nick Redfern, author of *Three Men Seeking Monsters*, and numerous other books on paranormal topics, agrees. In his article "Lair of the Beasts: Bigfoot: The Problem of Food" he states:

> Many researchers of the Bigfoot phenomenon take the view that the hairy, man-like beasts are some form of unknown ape. ... I, however, do not. ... Indeed, it's fair to say I think Bigfoot is a beast of paranormal – rather than flesh and blood – origins. There's a good reason I say that. It has to do with Bigfoot's eating habits. Or, more correctly, it's lack of eating habits. ... – a major problem when it comes to suggesting Bigfoot is just an ape and not something much weirder, and perhaps even phantom-like.

In our fast paced world we're continually presented with technological marvels. We live in a time where virtually anything is possible and monumental change happens with accustomed regularity; in fact, *it's expected.* The discovery of new planets is now met with a yawn. Could it be that the notion of Bigfoot has become so ubiquitous within our culture that we're collectively *creating* Bigfoot? Is Bigfoot a type of cultural phantasm? Maybe we are slowly habituating ourselves to the idea that Bigfoot is real to the point where its discovery (in some form or another) is imminent. The same could be said for UFOs. If so, one would assume this would hold true in other cases. Perhaps demons, vampires, and werewolves were a reality to people during the Dark Ages until they were told they didn't exist, effectively removing them from their (and our) reality. Right now Bigfoot remains hazy, like a pixilated digital photo that hasn't fully loaded, but given time it may emerge into our dimension with crystal clarity.

Is it possible the inhabitants of Van Meter unintentionally *revised* their reality for a brief few nights allowing something otherworldly and nightmarish to momentarily take form? Perhaps it took the form of something lurking within the town's subconscious, something plucked out of their distant memories and cultural background. Many of Van Meter's early settlers were of German descent and far less distanced from their Old World customs than the population is today. Like many cultures, German folklore is filled with stories involving supernatural creatures that inhabit the rivers, hills, and woods.

One of these creatures is the *Habergeiss* (or *Haferbock* depending on the region), a creature with roots throughout Germany and Austria. In Pagan times the Habergeiss was a spirit of the fields known as the "Goat of the Oats." It was called up in the autumn to help ensure a bountiful harvest. After the arrival of Christianity, the Habergeiss was disfigured and transformed into a kind of demon, as was the fate many Pagan gods and spirits. The Habergeiss is typically described as a ghostly, man-sized, horned, birdlike creature with three legs and a face like a goat. According to legend it would make odd sounds and moan at night, an indicator that someone was about to die. Needless to say, it was a very bad omen.

The Habergeiss was also known to attack cattle and drain them of blood. This is interesting, as it mirrors contemporary reports of cattle mutilations which often follow UFO and mysterious animal (cryptid) sightings. Is it possible that an alien intelligence chose this form after tapping into the folk memories of the people of Van Meter? Or was it an eerie relic from the Old World, an ancient wraith hitchhiking inside the collective psyche of the residents hoping to gain a foothold in a new land. The timing is also interesting. The Habergeiss is an autumnal spirit. According to reports, the Van Meter Visitor appeared in the last week of September shortly after the Autumnal Equinox on September 24th 1903 and terrorized the town during the nights leading up to the Harvest Moon on October 6. Like the Habergeiss, it was large, horned, and birdlike. It also made strange and eerie sounds at night. The Van Meter Visitor was reported by O.V. White as making a sound like "two rasps being rubbed together" and by Peter Dunn as sounding like "someone strangling." Later, according to J.B. Pratt, it made "peculiar sounds" from the abandoned mine. Was the 'Goat of the Oats' seeking its annual sacrifice that autumn in Van Meter, Iowa? One thing is certain: something very weird, and moderately rare, occurred there in the fall of 1903.

Daimonic Reality

Ultraterrestrials could be the same mythological monsters our ancestors warned us of in folktales. They were brought to life in otherworldly paintings and venerated by etching their likeness into stone monuments. In his book, *UFOs: Operation Trojan Horse* (1970) John Keel discovered some interesting clues after studying books on demonology and occult studies, stating:

> The manifestations and occurrences described in this imposing literature are similar if not entirely identical to the UFO phenomenon itself. ... thousands of books have been written on the subject of demonology which is the ancient and scholarly study of monsters and demons. The manifestations and occurrences described in this literature are identical to the UFO phenomenon. Victims of demonic possession suffer from the same medical and emotional symptoms as the UFO contactee. ... The UFO manifestations seem to be, by and large, merely minor variations of the age-old demonological phenomenon.

Jacques Vallee agreed in his book *Messengers of Deception* (1979) when he writes, "[An] impressive parallel could be made between UFO occupants and the popular conception of demons." He continues this hypothesis further in *Confrontations: A Scientist's Search for Alien Contact* (1990) saying, "The belief pattern that has been created around UFO abductions is reminiscent of medieval theories of abduction by demons, pacts with Satan, and the witches' Sabbat, complete with the Mark of the Devil on the body of the witch." This indicates that mankind has had contact with strange beings for a very long time.

The theory is explored in-depth by author and philosopher Patrick Harpur in his book, *Daimonic Reality: A Field Guide to the Other World* (2003). It is a brilliant work and essential reading for anyone interested the paranormal field. Harpur draws upon Carl Jung's psychological theories and Neoplatonist philosophy to arrive at what he calls the "Daimonic reality" theory. These are not the Christian "demons" many are familiar with. The term "demon" stems from the Greek word "daimon," referring to intelligences that existed somewhere between our physical world and the world of spirit. Their forms were often representative of human desires, dreams, inspirations, anxieties, and fears (what we would today call inner psychological principles), resulting in symbolic and archetypal manifestations including: dryads, nymphs, satyrs, titans, and other phantasmagoric creatures. They were thought to provide an essential link between the gods and men–intermediary agents between the celestial and material worlds. Later, this Greco-Roman bestiary was converted into "demons" by Christianity, along with elves, trolls, gnomes, etc. However, they are not simple messengers or trans-dimensional couriers. To this point Harpur makes an important distinction when he states, "They did not have to convey the message; they were themselves the message."

He continues by suggesting the entities originate from within the *Anima Mundi*, or "World Soul," a realm of consciousness encompassing all things and existing betwixt the world of matter and world of spirit. Like Talbot's Holographic Theory, Hurpur theorizes that our physical world is nothing more than a projection (or manifestation) of the "World Soul," a crystallization of thoughts. In essence, they are us and we are they; any appearance of separateness is merely illusion. Harpur writes, "Never quite divine nor quite human, the daimons erupted out of the Soul of the World. They were neither spiritual nor physical, but both. Neither were they, as Jung discovered, wholly inner nor wholly outer, but both. They were paradoxical beings, both good and bad, benign and frightening, guiding and warning, protecting and maddening." With this Harpur appears to indicate that our "personal demons" may be a lot more real than we realize.

What he is suggesting is when inexplicable events happen: crop circles, sightings of lake monsters, the appearance of alien spacecraft, etc. it is because we are performing a type of unconscious theurgical feat, making an object manifest, however briefly, until it collapses under the weight of the laws of what we generally consider objective *consensus* reality. In Quantum Mechanics this is called "objective collapse." They appear strange because they don't fit well into the context of our reality, but what if we are actually doing this all the time? Allow me to give you an example: If one wants a job or promotion badly one's will or desire to attain it often manifests in the physical world as increased productivity, or perhaps a return to school for further training. Once one receives the job or promotion it is usually chalked up to hard work and fortitude—all physical accomplishments—forgetting that it was one's initial conscious will to make the needed changes in the first place. Perhaps, like a controlled madness, we are consciously and *unconsciously* changing the world around us all the time; it's only when those changes appear strange or seemingly impossible that we really sit up and take notice. According to Keel, "UFOmania is no different than demonomania. ... We are meant to be crazy. It is an important part of the human condition. ... This planet is haunted by us; the other occupants just evade boredom by filling our skies and seas with monsters."

Tricksters, Cosmic Clowns, and Chaos

Another theory similar to the Daimonic Reality Theory is the "Trickster Theory," wonderfully examined by George P. Hanson in *The Trickster and the Paranormal*, one of the best books on paranormal research written in decades. Hanson worked on paranormal research at the Rhine Research Center in Durham, NC for eight years and has published a number of academic papers on the subject. After years of study, Hanson began wondering why it was so difficult to reproduce paranormal activity in a controlled laboratory setting even though it appears to be a fairly regular occurrence worldwide. Regardless of the current popularity of "ghost-hunting" television shows, the fact remains that after over a century of psychical research we are no closer to understanding the nature of paranormal events.

Harpur also wondered why parapsychology is continually plagued by odd and improbable incidents and why it has remained marginalized by the general scientific community. He believes the culprit is the "Trickster" phenomena (or principle). Referring to this dilemma he states:

> Psi phenomena, including synchronicities, are somewhat "ideoplastic," that is, they respond to, and are shaped by, the ideas, beliefs, and anxieties of the observers – a fact demonstrated in both laboratory and field studies. The phenomena also display a measure of intelligence. This is unlike most natural sciences, which deal primarily with non-conscious entities. When an investigator studies something that can be intentionally deceitful, and has intelligence-gathering capabilities of its own, the usual paradigms of science are inadequate. New frameworks and perspectives are needed.

The Trickster phenomena can be extremely daunting—even adversarial—when it manifests through series of unfortunate events or extreme cases of bad luck. Incidents of mysterious "battery-drain," malfunctioning equipment, or even just plain old carelessness are a well known phenomenon among paranormal researchers, ufologists, and amateur ghost hunters. In fact, it is practically *expected.* Camera or car batteries mysteriously go dead; gadgets and meters refuse to work properly; memory disks become corrupted, though one of the most frustratingly common problems is simple forgetfulness. People have otherworldly experiences, yet it never occurs to them to grab a video camera or snap a picture—*even when they were holding a camera right in their hand the whole time!* Only later do they wonder: *Why didn't I take a picture?* I am guilty of this myself.

A few years ago I interviewed a man who claimed he saw a UFO hovering over his neighborhood. A few workmen working on the road nearby saw it too. He described it as large, saucer-shaped, metallic, and silent. He said they all watched it hover for at least fifteen minutes. Never once did he think to run and grab a camera. Neither did the workmen. The man concluded the story by saying, "Since it wasn't doing anything I eventually got bored and went back inside to watch television." Bored! Is this a normal reaction after witnessing something utterly extraordinary? I certainly hope not. Though it is possible he was subject to the hypnotic affect of ultraterrestrial contact. Perhaps our brains are temporarily affected just like electronics. We become entranced or stupefied by what we are witnessing. Or perhaps it is a form of hypnosis.

Hanson theorizes that paranormal activity is the result of a "trickster principle" at work in the universe. By using the term "Trickster," Hansdon does not imply that the phenomenon is the result of some kind puckish entity that enjoys playing bizarre pranks on mystified mortals; instead, he theorizes it is a kind of cosmic force or law like gravity. Some call it a cosmic farce. However, whereas gravity is a law that attracts, the Trickster is a law confounds. It bewilders, breaks down logic, and is utterly irrational.

When dealing with the Trickster nothing is what it seems, for the Trickster is also a tutelary force. If you look at all the trickster gods of the world's mythologies: Hermes of the Greeks, Loki of the Norse, Eshu-Elegba of the West African Yoruban tribe, and Coyote of many Native American tribes, they are all invariably portrayed as shape-shifters and are paradoxically both cunning and foolish. Trickster gods typically come off as untrustworthy, even clownish; they are never what they seem. However, their mad antics only serve as a mask for deeper wisdom or hidden knowledge. They are masters of misdirection and cruel irony, but those with keen perception can see past their obfuscation and are rewarded with new and profound understanding, though more often than not, humans who interact with them tend to learn this the hard way.

Hanson describes their paradoxical nature when he states, "Tricksters are marginal characters; they live at boundaries, with uncertain, ambiguous statuses." Through transformation Tricksters personify a duality of opposites: material and spiritual, male and female, clumsy and deft, profane and holy, foolish and wise. In so doing, like the Greek daimons, they serve as a link between our material realm, often considered lowly, and the lofty realm of spirit. Hanson adds, "Tricksters are boundary crossers; they destabilize structures; they govern transitions. They also embody paradox, contradiction, and ambiguity." Again, he is not insinuating that Tricksters are mischievous sentient entities (or gods), rather, they spontaneously erupt from our own collective consciousness, and if we pay close enough attention, we can learn something about ourselves.

Artist's interpretation of the Van Meter Visitor
(Art work by Kevin Lee Nelson)

The Unified Theory

All these theories, which are really just variations of a common theme, point to a potential *unified theory* of paranormal events. For the sake of convenience, I will use John Keel's term, *ultraterrestrial*, as it succinctly sums up the basic nature and potential origin of the phenomena. Furthermore, his theory is broad enough to allow for the basic tenets of all the other theories mentioned above.

According to the Ultraterrestrial Theory, Bigfoot, lake monsters, phantoms, UFOs, elves, and winged beasts (as in the Van Meter case) could *all* be ultraterrestrials. They paradoxically originate from both within our minds and from (what we perceive to be) outside them. They have material reality but are also projections of consciousness, as our own physical bodies may very well be. Still, the features of ultraterrestrials are not entirely random. They do exhibit a few common traits. This is not surprising, as cultures worldwide also share a number of common folkloric features and themes. Creation myths are surprisingly similar around the world, as are tales of dragons for example. The dragon-boats of the Vikings share striking characteristics to ancient Chinese carvings. It may be possible to attribute such phenomena to our early ancestors' fears, namely, fear of natural disasters and large nocturnal predators. Could it be possible that persistent racial anxieties, which have been with us for millennia, occasionally reach a tipping point or critical mass–a calcification of consciousness—whereby they break through into our physical reality?

Uncommon Traits

Let us now explore a few tell-tale characteristics common among ultraterrestrial reports, and how these compare to the events surrounding the Van Meter Visitor case. This can be a daunting task, for according to the ultraterrestrial theory these entities can appear in almost any form: winged beasts, aliens, phantoms, angels, creatures from folklore, odd human beings—even intelligent machines. Their traits are extremely varied making it difficult to define and categorize; however, they do have a few things in common.

Baffling Behavior

Ultraterrestrials almost always behave in a very strange and inexplicable manner. For example, when manifesting in a human-like form they often exhibit inexplicable and befuddling behavior to those who encounter them, making them stand out. The classic "Men in Black" phenomenon is considered by many to be a specific guise of ultraterrestrials, perhaps one that stems from distrust of government agencies. They are often reported to drive cars that are out of date by decades, use old fashioned expressions like "23 skidoo," "the cat's pajamas," or "don't take any wooden nickels." They also dress oddly, usually wearing clothes that fit poorly; either too short or too loose, and that is long out of fashion. This is one of the most common hallmarks of ultraterrestrials, whether they appear as a person or as a phantasmal being: they always behave oddly and seem out of place.

Sometimes it appears that even natural laws, like the laws of physics, do not apply to them, such as their apparent inability to be harmed. In cases where they *do* appear harmed, or even killed, their bodies mysteriously vanish like a figment from a dream, leaving no evidence, like the famous Minnesota Ice Man or the Roswell UFO crash. One of the best recently documented cases of ultraterrestrial contact is documented in the book, *The Hunt for the Skinwalker* by Colm A. Kelleher and George Knapp. Among dozens of eye-witness encounters detailed in the book, one in particular describes an encounter with an enormous wolf-like creature on a remote ranch in Utah. The wolf casually walked up to group of people on the ranch, seemingly unafraid. At first it appeared friendly, and they were all mildly amused by its strange behavior. Then it suddenly attacked a young calf in a nearby pen. A few of the men savagely kicked the wolf to make it release the calf, yet it seemed unconcerned and refused to let go. Finally, one of the men unloaded four .357 magnum rounds into the wolf at close range. It had no effect whatsoever. "It didn't yelp, didn't pause, and didn't bleed." Eventually it let go. It was shot a few more times with a thirty aught six. Chunks of flesh came off, yet the wolf was unfazed. Finally it trotted off, apparently unharmed, with an air of utter indifference towards both its wounds and the ranchers.

This incident in some ways mirrors the encounter with the Van Meter Visitor. A skilled marksman shot the creature at close range, yet it appeared unharmed, as if the bullets passed right through it. Perhaps these creatures are not entirely material, or not quite in phase with our reality, making them somewhat intangible and not subject to same limitations as earthy matter. Yet they are still corporeal enough to interact with and affect our environment, like attacking the calf, or in the Van Meter case, the creature was able to "climb down a telephone pole using its beak like a parrot."

Roads Less Traveled

As the old hackneyed real-estate phrase goes, "There are three things that matter in property: location, location, location." Ultraterrestrial activity is no different. Location is a very important and perhaps *essential* feature in most ultraterrestrial encounters. It has been observed by many researchers that most incidents occur in locations sharing a few common features or functions; most important of these being their borderline quality, places on the periphery, also known as *liminal* spaces. It is not known whether these beings prefer these locations or if the locations themselves somehow assist in or even generates their manifestation. Keel writes, "In earlier times fairies, demons, and even human witches practicing their Black Sabbath rites, chose gravel pits, garbage dumps, cemeteries, and crossroads for their appearances. Modern hairy monsters and UFOs select the same sites…"

One could also add bridges, deep pools & wells, caves/mines, and sacred mounds to that list. It is at forlorn and forgotten places, and in-between spaces, that the fabric of reality is the most threadbare, allowing beings from other dimensions (or time) to occasionally slip through. These are points of trans-dimensional intersection, where two or more different dimensions or realities intersect or occupy the same space, and where things are not always as they seem. Cultures around the world have always acknowledged these unusual places, usually designating them as either sacred or cursed…a place to be revered or shunned. Today they go by many names: portals, vortices, nexus points, geomantic power sites, or simply "soft spots" in our reality. It is in these places that anomalous events and ultraterrestrial contact is most likely to occur.

Intersection points are considered "liminal" areas, because they exist partly in this reality and partly in another, like a bridge spanning dimensions. The term "liminal" stems from the word "limen," meaning "threshold," and was first coined by French ethnographer and folklorist Arnold Van Gennep in his book *The Rites of Passage* (1909). Liminality suggests the blurring of boundaries. It is a zone that is neither here nor there, but simultaneously both. To give a folkloric example, Halloween and Walpurgisnacht (May Eve) are considered liminal nights. Both are nights where the dead are thought to inhabit the same world as the living. Each night also occurs at the end of a season and beginning of another. Halloween was the Celtic New Year and marked the end of the summer harvest and beginning of winter. *Walpurgisnacht*, or Beltane, marked the end of winter and beginning of the spring planting season. Both were considered auspicious nights because they were nights of transition, instability, and represented a brief period of time that is seasonally ambiguous.

In *The Trickster and the Paranormal,* Hanson explains how liminal zones and psychical activity are dual-natured, unpredictable, and not subject to conventional logic. Instead, they obey a kind of "meta-logic," a term used by Vallee to describe an advanced form of reasoning that is so far beyond our comprehension that it appears absurd and random to our contemporary brains. Referring to UFOs in particular Harpur writes, "UFO phenomena are fundamentally liminal, interstitial, betwixt and between, and anti-structural. UFOs inhabit the realm between heaven and earth (a binary position), much like spirits and angels, and they share common properties with them. In this domain we also find a blurring of imagination and reality, another binary opposition."

This is one of the key reasons why psychical events and paranormal phenomena are nearly impossible to study and observe under laboratory conditions. They seem to operate under their own mysterious set of rules, breaking down the rational into the irrational. Hanson explains, "…psi, the paranormal, and the supernatural are fundamentally linked to deconstructing change, transition, disorder, marginality, the ephemera, fluidity, ambiguity, and blurring of boundaries." It appears the scientific method is ill-equipped to tackle such a beast. The phenomenon is too ephemeral. It amounts to trying to catch smoke with a butterfly net.

So is Van Meter, Iowa, located at one of these liminal zones and caught between dimensions? Or if not now, was it in 1903? There is reason to believe that liminal zones are somewhat fixed and static. Many of the world's sacred sites are believed to be located at such places: early shamans and priests were guided to places of power to erect megaliths; religious visionaries and mystics were instructed by mysterious messengers to build churches at specific holy locations (often building over earlier sacred sites); contemporary psychics and highly intuitive people sense these "soft spots" and make regular pilgrimages and seek their preservation. These are sites where sensitive individuals can have direct contact with the numinous, where one can get a sense of another world, and occasionally get a glimpse of its inhabitants.

Liminal zones can also be considered psychogeographical in nature, meaning they exist within a psychological landscape. The term also refers to
features within the physical terrain which trigger certain moods, atmos-
pheres, and induce psychological effects in those within the radius of their
influence. One could say that liminal zones form the peaks and valleys of
a mental topography and are part of a landscape comprised of intuition-
based landmarks—a panorama observed by the sixth sense.

There are a few key features and traits all these sites have in common. Tra-
ditionally the most common factor was a crossroads, the crossing (or merg-
ing into a 'Y') of two or more roads or rivers—anything that can conduct
traffic or allow the flow of energy currents, whatever that may be. Crossroads are liminal places, an intersection point that is neither this road nor
that, but both. They have been considered sites of power for millennia and
sacred to gods and goddesses like Hecate, Hermes, and Legba—all
gods/goddesses of the crossroads. It is also the place where, according to
legend, one makes demonic pacts or buries magical items. Famous Delta
Blues musician Robert Johnson allegedly sold his soul to the Devil at a
crossroads so that he could play guitar like the Devil himself. Johnson perhaps regretted it later, writing songs like *Hellhound On My Trail*. According to legend, he paid the price and gave the Devil his due. He only lived
to be 29.

Not surprisingly, Van Meter sits at a crossroads. At Van Meter, the Raccoon
River splits into two rivers (the Raccoon River and the Middle Raccoon
River). This division was further crossed by a road in 1903. Today Hwy
80 spans the spot. In fact, the mine, reported home of the strange creature,
sits directly below the area where the rivers and road converge.

However, what if not all crossroads are visible? There is a theory that the
surface of the earth is covered by an intricate web of energy paths that
conduct a flow of telluric energy. This idea was first proposed by Alfred
Watkins in his 1921 book, *Early British Trackways*. He referred to these
"straight tracks" as the "ley," what some now call "ley lines" or "spirit
roads." Places where the ley intersect are believed to be exceptionally po-
tent. The greater the number of intersections, the greater the site's telluric
power. Extreme examples include Glastonbury Tor, Sedona, the Bermuda
Triangle, Ayers Rock, Machu Picchu, and the Great Pyramid.

The name "ley" comes from the discovery that many of the energy roads passed through places with names containing the syllable "ley." The paths tend to leave tell-tale signs along their routes, most notably in the names of people and places. It has been noted by John Mitchell in his book *The View Over Atlantis* (and later by John Keel in *The Mothman Prophesies*) that, "A peculiar feature of the old alignments is that certain names appear with remarkable frequency along their routes. Names with Red, White, and Black are common; so are Cold or Cole, Dod, Merry, and Ley." Interestingly, the first physician and druggist of Van Meter was C.M. Dodge. Dodge is an Anglo-Saxon name that is derived from the baptismal name *Dod*. Furthermore, one of the eyewitnesses of the Van Meter Visitor was O.V. *White*. A building carrying his name can be seen on the cover of this book. As you can see, Van Meter had the signs, or what some call *symptoms*, of being located along one of the legendary spirit roads.

Liminal sites typically act as "ground zero" for all sorts of paranormal activity. Areas reporting repeated UFO sightings also tend to have a large number of allegedly haunted locations and reports of other bizarre phenomenon. Van Meter is no exception. Of course nearly every town has a house rumored to be haunted; this is not unusual, but for a small town with a population of barely over a thousand souls it has an abnormally large number of hauntings and anomalous sightings. One might say that Van Meter is *overrepresented.*

Hellmouth blocked by an angel
(Winchester Psalter – 12th century)

One allegedly haunted site is the old high school. Most of the ghostly activity seems to occur in the old gymnasium. Local legend states that a young girl tragically died after falling from the balcony and is now believed to haunt the place. While in Van Meter we spoke with several employees of the school, including the janitor, who reported seeing and hearing odd things late at night while the school is empty.

Another example is a downtown tavern called Fat Randi's Bar and Grill which some believe is haunted. The individuals we spoke to said most of the paranormal activity takes place in the basement. Doors have been known open and close on their own and toilets flush by themselves. The owner believes the spirit is a woman, but no real cause for the haunting is known.

Then of course there are the ruins of the brick factory, mentioned in an earlier chapter, which has a long-standing reputation for being haunted. Not much remains of the factory today. It sits just a short distance from where the entrance to the mine used to be. When we spoke to the current landowner he recalled how spooky it was when he used to camp out at night near the old factory. He reported hearing strange sounds late at night that were unlike any animal he knew.

When one adds local stories about the river monster inhabiting the Raccoon River and other tales of hairy werewolf or Bigfoot-like creatures, one begins to get the feeling that there is something peculiar about area around Van Meter. This is fairly typical of liminal zones. One might say they are psychically *porous*. When an area is not watertight to the pressure exerted by other dimensions one is bound to get leaks.

Winged Messengers

As mentioned before, ultraterrestrials come in all shapes and sizes, including some that are truly bizarre. In one report from the case at Skinwalker Ranch a possible ultraterrestrial is described as a floating "refrigerator looking vehicle" covered in white and red lights that flew away into the sky when they tried to approach it. Nonetheless, the vast majority of reports describe large humanoid creatures with wings and bird-like (or bat-like) qualities.

The famous Mothman of Point Pleasant, West Virginia is perhaps one of the most emblematic of these. The Mothman was seen by scores of witnesses around Point Pleasant over the weeks leading up to the Silver Bridge collapse that killed 46 people on December 15th 1967. Keel states, "Altogether, more than one hundred adults would see this winged impossibility in 1966-67. Those who got a close look at it all agreed on the basic points. It was gray, apparently featherless, as large—or larger—than a big man, had a wingspan of about ten feet, took off straight up like a helicopter, and did not flap its wings in flight." One of the witnesses, Marvin Shock, reported multiple creatures that "looked about as big as a man would look moving about trees. ... a wingspread of at least ten feet ... their breasts were gray and they had five-or-six inch bills, straight, not curved like those of hawks or vultures." Witness Mervyn Hutchinson described it as "looking like a human-sized bat, with big bat wings on its back." Point Pleasant was inundated with sightings of winged creatures, many of which were spotted near an abandoned ammunition dump, a liminal spot. What Keel didn't realize when he wrote *The Mothman Prophesies* was that the people of Van Meter, Iowa were visited by an eerily similar creature over sixty years *before* the incidents at Point Pleasant.

Winged humanoids have ancient roots going all the way back to the Egyptians and the Babylonians. Western culture has been continually fascinated by them, usually in the form of divine messengers, such as the biblical Seraphim and Cherubim. Ezekiel 10:12-14 (KJV) has perhaps the most phantasmagoric description of the winged Cherubim, "And their whole body, and their backs, and their hands, and their wings, and the wheels, were full of eyes round about, ... And every one had four faces: the first face was the face of a cherub, and the second face was the face of a man, and the third the face of a lion, and the fourth the face of an eagle." Here we have a creature with wings, multi-faced (including a bird-face), and *with wheels?* This description perfectly describes the chimeric nature of the ultraterrestrial: a being exhibiting traits of birds, beasts, and men— *even machines.*

Terrestrial traits melded with avian traits reflect the dual nature of ultraterrestrials. It is an expression of their liminal status. Their transitional appearance is symbolic of the ambiguity of their existence in the spaces between worlds. It is also possible that their true form is impossible for our brains to comprehend having no physical context or reference point within the mundane world. Thus, our brains make poor attempts to fill in the gaps by utilizing traits we are already familiar with: birds, people, machines, etc., which amounts to a mishmash of incongruent and often nightmarish characteristics. Nearly one hundred years ago famous horror writer H.P. Lovecraft wrote, "The most merciful thing in the world, I think, is the inability of the human mind to correlate all its contents. We live on a placid island of ignorance in the midst of black seas of infinity, and it was not meant that we should voyage far." I think he understood better than most just how limited our ability to truly understand of the cosmos (and reality) really is. Human understanding is restricted by our five senses and bound by the limits of our cognitive ability. What our brains interpret as "wings" might be a feature that is actually far, *far,* stranger. So perhaps for our sake it is a good thing that we are *only* seeing bird-like creatures.

A Language From Beyond

According to witnesses, ultraterrestrials frequently attempt communication either though strange sounds, verbally, or even psychically. As mentioned before, verbal communication is typically marked by odd speech patterns. Sometimes their choice of words may seem archaic or their voices are unusually squeaky and high-pitched for their body size. It's interesting that folklore describes elves and fairies as having "silvery voices" that are high, quick, beguiling, and sweet. A contemporary example would be the comical voices of "Alvin and the Chipmunks," created by sped-up voice recordings. In fact, in *The Mothman Prophesies* Keel notes,

> ...their rapid-fire unintelligible 'language' noted by witnesses all over the world as sounding like "a speeded up phonograph record" could be caused by their failure to adjust to our time cycle when they enter our space-time continuum. They are talking at a faster rate because their time is different from ours. When they manage to adjust, they have to forcibly slow themselves down, articulating their words slowly, in a singsong manner.

In other cases they're completely unintelligible, just bizarre noises. Keel states, "Entities have a logic system quite different from ours and when they try to translate things on our level their statements come out absurd." One of the Mothman witnesses, Mrs. Virginia Thomas, described the squeaking sound made by the Mothman as, "like a bad fan belt...but much louder." She later had a prophetic dream about the Silver Bridge collapse.

In the Van Meter case the mysterious visitor was reported as sounding like a metallic grating sound, the sound of a person choking, or just plain "peculiar." This could be the result of some kind of distortion, like a radio transmission partly obscured by static. The reason for the distortion is anyone's guess, as is their motivation for contact. One may presume that disruptions in space-time warp sound waves. Or perhaps their vocal organs are suited to their native dimension, a place far different than ours.

One wonders if the Van Meter Visitor was attempting communication, or if it was a breed of transdimensional wildlife mistakenly transported through a rift in time and space. On the surface the Visitor did not behave in a manner than would suggest a high degree of intelligence, at least as we understand it. That said; it is important to realize that its appearance and behavior may have been a rouse, or an implanted projection, as discussed earlier. The people of Van Meter were familiar with birds and bats, so the creature may have used what they knew, taking on characteristics of each.

An acquaintance of mine, C. Williams, recently described a truly bizarre incident involving his brother Shawn who may have heard ultraterrestrial "language" one night while walking his dog. The incident occurred one night in 2012 at a dog park in Madison, Wisconsin. Mr. Williams said:

> It was about 10:30 pm so the park was closed, and Shawn figured no one was there. While walking his dog he heard what sounded like an Asian lady calling her dog or something, he couldn't understand what she was saying. Then she said, "Shawn can you pick up my phone? Shawn will you answer my phone?" changing it each time like that. He was going to say, "Are you talking to me?" but when he looked back he saw what he said didn't really look like a person, and it was moving from side to side faster than a person could, plus he said the things it was saying got faster and it never took a breath. He took off running to the lake.

Mysterious Lights

A brilliant flash of light or an intense focused beam aimed at the observer is a familiar feature one finds again and again when researching ultraterrestrial encounters. Witnesses often report strange hypnotic lights that may induce temporary paralysis. Many have described it as feeling like a deer in the headlights—transfixed to the spot. Keel describes the phenomena by stating:

> ...the experience usually begins with either the sudden flash of light or a sound – a humming, buzzing, or beeping. The subject's attention is riveted to a pulsing, flickering light of dazzling intensity. He finds he is unable to move a muscle and is rooted to the spot.

The events in Van Meter began with U.G. Griffith seeing something that looked like an "electric search light" on a nearby rooftop which then flew over to another rooftop and disappeared. The following night Dr. Allcot saw what he described as a "bright light" that dazzled and "nearly blinded him". Upon investigation he discovered the source of the light was a large humanoid creature with bat-like wings. He describes the light as emitting from a "blunt horn-like protuberance" from the middle of the Visitor's forehead. Again the following night Peter Dunn saw the winged creature and was "blinded by the presence of a light of great intensity."

What kind of animal could emit a bright light? One very hypothetical theory could be that the Platt mine in Van Meter (a shaft 257 feet deep) broke into a closed subterranean ecosystem releasing an unknown bat-like creature to the upper world (and the others spotted at the mouth of the mine). They may have been an evolutionary offshoot or a surviving species from the distant past. This may sound like a real stretch, but it is not without precedent. In 2006 quarry workers in Israel discovered Ayyalon cave which had been completely sealed from the outside world for *millions* of years and stretched 330 feet deep. Inside the cave they found a thriving and totally independent ecosystem, including four undiscovered species of water-dwelling crustaceans and four land-dwelling invertebrates.

Another possible factor, albeit remote, is the extremely high levels of radon in the area. Iowa bedrock has the largest concentrations of radon in the nation. Radon is a known carcinogen. Could high levels of radon trapped beneath the earth be a possible cause for extreme mutations? The University of Minnesota's School of Public Health website has advisories about Radon radiation exposure stating, "When an alpha particle passes through a cell nucleus, DNA is likely to be damaged. More specifically, available data indicates that alpha particle penetration of the cell nucleus may cause genomic changes typically in the form of point mutations and transformations."

So is it possible the Van Meter creatures were mutant animals that used bioluminescence to navigate caverns deep under the earth? As intriguing as this all sounds, it is highly doubtful. Even animals capable of bioluminescence, like fireflies or deep-sea anglerfish, are only able to give off a low-intensity glow—certainly nothing close to an electric search light. Furthermore, the Visitor was described as being eight feet tall. It is highly unlikely there would be an adequate food source deep underground to support such a large creature. This makes it highly improbably that whatever descended on Van Meter was an undiscovered flesh-and-blood animal, but rather something completely alien; perhaps even alien to our dimension.

Bright lights have always been synonymous with all sorts of paranormal activity. We could go all the way back to our earlier biblical account from Ezekiel. A description of angelic entities in Ezekiel 1:13 (KJV) reads, "As for the likeness of the living creatures, their appearance was like burning coals of fire, and like the appearance of lamps: it went up and down among the living creatures; and the fire was bright, and out of the fire went forth lightning." Those who see angels often describe them as appearing within a column of celestial fire or emitting a brilliant and heavenly luminescence.

UFO reports and alien abduction cases almost always include descriptions of strange lights or blinding beams. Everyone is familiar with the image of spacecraft shining a column of light or "tractor beams" down on helpless abductees. Again, in *The Mothman Prophesies* Keel points out just how ubiquitous this phenomena is, stating, "If you review the thousands of UFO contact reports you will find that many of them begin with the appearance of an entity holding some kind of "flashlight" which is shone directly at the witness." Sound familiar? He continues to make the connection between monstrous bird sightings and mysterious lights by stating:

> These great Garudas and winged beings are closely associated with luminous phenomena. They tend to appear in areas where UFOs have been active and, like UFOs, they tend to linger for days or even weeks in the same specific area. The big luminous bird of the Illinois-St.

Louis region in 1948 was visiting an area of the Mississippi valley that would see continuous UFO and hairy
monster activity thereafter.

In European folklore so-called "fairy-forts" are reported to be lit up by
strange lights on certain nights of the year. The mysterious lights, sometimes called "Ingneous Fatuuous" (meaning "fool's fire"), "will-o'-the-
whisp," or "friar's lanterns" are well known to lure curious onlookers out
into dangerous bogs and putting them in peril. In many states, one may
hear tales of mysterious and ghostly "spook lights," like the Marfa lights
in Texas, the Paulding light in Upper Michigan, and the Brown Mountain
lights in North Carolina that haunt lonely stretches of road. They hover in
the air and sometimes appear to move about with purpose. Colorful stories
explaining the origin of the light are usually plentiful in each case, such
as the lost soul of a train conductor who was tragically killed and now
haunts the region, forever searching with his spectral lantern. Like mischievous elves, the lights always remain at a distance, teasing the viewer,
and often disappear entirely if one gets too close.

What is the purpose of these dazzling displays? Do they serve as warnings
in the same way flashing railroad crossing lights caution us of danger
ahead? Or perhaps the opposite; they could they be radiant lures, beckon-
ing us for some unknown reason like moths to a flame. Are they produced
by a form of advanced technology—a type of weapon emitting a trance-
inducing ray? Perhaps in some cases the light could it be a visual reaction
generated by our brains in response to witnessing something shocking or
when gaining a glimpse of another dimension. When one is struck hard
on the back of the head one often sees a white flash across their vision.
Could the brilliant light be a physical reaction to otherworldly contact, a
form of *psychic* pummeling, or exposure to an unknown form of radiation?
Interestingly, many witnesses report physical side-effects after an encounter mirroring symptoms of radiation exposure, such as conjunctivitis
(bloodshot eyes) lasting for days; fingernails may darken, turn yellow, or
become brittle; skin may burn and peel like bad sunburn.

Brimstone in the Air

Yet another peculiar feature of ultraterrestrials is their incredible stench.
Encounters often include mention of a very unpleasant and lingering smell.
It is often described as having the distinctive "rotten egg" smell of burning

sulfur. In fact, one Florida's famous most famous monsters, the elusive "Skunk Ape" got its name because of its powerful odor. Sightings are usually preceded by a terrible and overpowering smell. In referring to ultraterrestrials, Keel writes, "…they are usually accompanied by the smell of rotten eggs—hydrogen sulfide. The 'fire and brimstone' of the ancients. The same odor frequently surrounds the fabled flying saucers and their space-suited pilots." When Dr. Allcot spotted the Visitor in Van Meter he was quoted as saying it had a "stupefying odor." The odor was so strong that it almost overcame him. So here again the Visitor fits another criteria for an ultraterrestrial encounter.

Today people often associate the smell of sulfur with demons, as many associate sulfur/brimstone with descriptions of Hell. This is actually a latter-day depiction and somewhat misleading; nevertheless, it's interesting how this all came about. You see, the biblical word for a hellish place (or just plain nasty) is "Gehenna," which is an English transliteration of the Greek form of the Aramaic word *ge hinnom*, meaning the "valley of Hinnom." It was an actual place, not just a theological threat. The Valley of Hinnom was basically Jerusalem's garbage dump. It was a steep valley just outside the city where people would dump trash, dead animals, and the bodies of criminals. It was also called Tophet—the valley of dead bones. They used sulfur (which burns for a long time and is very hard to extinguish once set alight) to keep the trash pit continually burning day and night. Here again we have liminal territory: a garbage dump, a graveyard, and a forlorn and avoided place on the outskirts of the city. This is the habitat of the ultraterrestrial. Obviously a valley full of noxious fumes and burning bodies would have been a dreadful sight. "Gehenna" became the local slang used for describing the worst place imaginable. Later the King James Bible changed and Saxonized the word "Gehenna" to "Hell," stemming from the northern European Pagan words for the underworld *hel, helle, hellja* etc. People confuse the metaphor, thinking "fire and brimstone" is an actual feature of Hell, confusing the map for the territory, as it were. Instead, heat and sulfur is used to describe what Hell is supposed to be like. Of course, there are many diverse interpretations of Hell. According to Dante's *Inferno*, the deepest level of hell, the Ninth Circle (reserved for traitors), is a *frozen lake*.

The mystery deepens when one looks at properties of sulfur in history, particularly in alchemy. Here again we find liminalty. Not surprisingly, according to alchemical texts sulfur is an element of dualities. It is an extremely unusual element in that it has masculine qualities, hot and dry, and feminine qualities, cold and moist. Like the ultraterrestrial it exists in and between two polarities. The symbol for sulfur, sometimes called "The Leviathan Cross" (see Figure 1) is a cipher.

This part gets a little heavy, so please bear with me. First, The Leviathan Cross contains an equilateral cross which is the sign of the crossroads representing a liminal zone. Within the symbol one may also notice the cross of the crucifixion. This shape is far more mystical than many realize. It is FAR more than just the shape of a Roman era execution device, as many assume. If one looks beyond the obvious surface meaning, one may notice the cross is a simplified 2D representation of something far more complex and profound. A cross is the shape you get when you unfold a cube and lay it flat. A cube represents dimensional space. We all know that a cube is bounded by six flat squares. However, in non-Euclidean geometry there is also a 4-dimenisional cube called a "tesseract" or "hypercube" (see Figure 3). A tesseract is a 2D representation of a 4-dimensional concept using a cube within a cube to represent the motion of two objects enfolding in upon each other with each form simultaneously occupying the same space. Whereas a standard 3-dimensional cube is bounded by six 2-dimensional squares, a 4-dimensional tesseract is bounded by eight 3-dimensional *cubes*. This too can be unfolded into a representation of a hyper-solid 4-dimensional shape as seen in Figure 4.

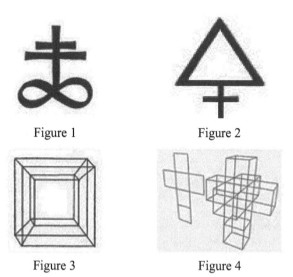

Figure 1   Figure 2

Figure 3   Figure 4

A tesseract is a representation of higher space and a means for one to gain a glimpse of the fourth dimension. Painter Salvidor Dali famously painted Christ on an unfolded tesseract in his painting, "Crucifixion." Cubist painter and theorist Albert Gleizes said, "Beyond the three dimensions of Euclid we have added another, the fourth dimension, which is to say, the figuration of space, the measure of the infinite." Thus, the cube, and its flat 2D representation, the cross, symbolize higher dimensions.

But the mystery doesn't stop there. The lower part of the sulfur symbol contains a Mobius Strip, looking like a figure eight turned on its side. This is the symbol for infinity. So within the symbol for sulfur we have coded representations of liminal space, multi-dimensionality, and timeless infinity. Is it any wonder ultraterrestrials are linked to this element? The other often-used alchemical symbol for sulfur is also telling. To use alchemical terminology, it is comprised of the "fire triangle" above the "cross of earth" (see Figure 2). Fire above earth...could this represent the reported "fire in the sky" created by UFOs and other anomalous phenomena? It gets even stranger. The atomic number of sulfur is 16. Using traditional Jewish Gematria, a system of assigning numerical value to a word or phrase, the number 16 equates to the phrases "clamorous bird" and also "to shine or gleam."

Too Many Coincidences?

Lastly, one of the most bewildering hallmarks of ultraterrestrial activity is the appearance of inexplicable synchronicities. It usually goes FAR beyond simple coincidence. Sometimes they get so frequent that people begin to think they are being sent coded messages, or even losing their mind. When ultraterrestrials are near, or when one is close of a liminal zone, synchronicities abound. Allow me to give you a personal example: a few years ago I was on a "legend trip" with my other two co-authors, Noah and Chad. The goal of our trip was to research and record legends and eye-witness reports about an alleged lake serpent thought to inhabit a lake in Wisconsin, and if we were lucky, maybe even catch a glimpse of it ourselves.

Over the course of our trip we began to notice that wherever we went we continually encountered songs by the 80s rock band The Police. At first none of us mentioned it, thinking it was just a fluke or silly coincidence. Then it got spooky. It didn't matter where we were: a restaurant, bookshop, motel office, gas station—we were followed by the high tenor vocals of The Police's front man Sting. There was no rational explanation; believe me, we checked. It wasn't due to a reunion tour (that was in 2008). They hadn't just been inducted to the Rock Hall of Fame (that was in 2003). There was simply no reason for it. Finally it got to be ridiculous. After a day out on the lake (with no music around) we rolled into a gas station/convenience store to fill up and buy a few snacks. I turned to my companions and said, *How much do you want to bet The Police will be playing when we walk inside?* After the trip we'd had they weren't willing to take that bet. We walked in, and—you guessed it—The Police. It was about halfway through the song. But it gets weirder: the song lyrics made a reference to a lake monster, "Many miles away - Something crawls to the surface - Of a dark Scottish loch," naturally referring to The Loch Ness Monster. Keep in mind we had just gotten off the boat after a long day of searching for a lake monster. A chill ran down my spine when I realized which song it was. The name of the song? *Synchronicity II.*

When synchronicities occur it is wise to pay attention. We could be getting a message from beyond or from deep within our own psyche. Either way, many feel the transmission is loaded potentially valuable information, at least for those willing to take notice. It may appear as nonsense on the surface, but there is usually a message buried in there, hidden within the static. Through increased awareness one may be able to improve the signal-to-noise ratio, whereby one may glean important inside information about future events or receive illuminating insight shedding light upon their inner self.

14
What happened to the
Mysterious footprint?

by Chad Lewis

One of the most intriguing aspects of this case involves the mystery of what happened to the plaster cast that was taken of the odd three-toed foot-prints that were discovered by Peter Dunn. During the night, Mr. Dunn blasted out the bank's window in an attempt to kill the light-wielding monster that was aggressively searching for him. The next morning, when not one single piece of the creature was found, Mr. Dunn was reeling with self-doubt as he assessed his decision to fire on the beast, which accounted for the destruction of the window. Convinced that whatever was terrorizing him during the night was indeed real, Mr. Dunn began a check of the build-ing's perimeter where he discovered a series of bizarre-looking three-toed tracks. The *Des Moines Daily News* reported that a plaster cast was made of at least one of these strange footprints. So if Dunn did in fact make a plaster cast of the strange looking footprint, what became of it? Now, over 100 years after the fact, that question still remains unanswered, and while there are endless possibilities as to the fate of the footprint, we will focus on a few of the most likely outcomes.

Noah Voss holds an alleged Bigfoot cast. Could a plaster cast survive
100 years?

Certainly the footprint, and the bizarre story that accompanied it, would have generated an immense amount of curiosity and interest among the residents of the area. During this time period, entertainment options were very scarce, so people often turned to any strange and unusual animals, people, plants and objects to help fill the void. Usually anything out of the ordinary would be put on display at a local business, where curious visitors would be charged a nickel or dime in order to see the mysterious find. Many of the country's larger cities also had dime museums, where for 10 cents customers could gaze at a three-legged pig or brush up next to a living "giant" while browsing through an entire shop of puzzling curiosities. In the mid 1800s, the most famous dime museum in the world was that of P.T. Barnum's American Museum in New York, which at its height attracted over 15,000 people a day. If Van Meter followed suit, the footprints may have been placed on display at a local business or gathering spot, perhaps even inside the bank, where the incident took place. If the footprint was put on display or stored in a local business, it most likely would have been burned in the fire of 1911, which destroyed nearly all of downtown Van Meter.

P.T. Barnum's New York Museum

We also have to consider that the cast was given to a museum for analysis and/or safe keeping. Yet, as far as we know, Van Meter had no such museum, making it much more likely that the footprint would have been sent to the Iowa State Historical Society in Des Moines, which had opened a collection museum in 1892. In our quest to track down the footprint, we headed to Des Moines to see if the Iowa State Historical Museum had any similar items in its possession. We spoke with various employees from several departments, including archives, collections and museum education. Much to our surprise, no one had so much as even heard of the Van Meter case, and our hope that the footprint was safely tucked away in some storage area vanished in the span of an afternoon.

But what if the footprint never found its way into a museum? What if it was never put on display at a local gathering spot, but instead, it was simply stored away. Perhaps Mr. Dunn or someone else closely connected to the case wanted to keep it as a souvenir or as a visual reminder of the strange events that plagued their town. Following this line of reasoning, we decided to inquire about the footprint with as many area residents as possible. In October of 2012, recognizing the need for further information, we gave a lecture in Van Meter to share our research on the incident with the residents and, more importantly, to let them know what areas of the case that were still a mystery to us, hoping that someone may be able to fill in some of the gaps. The presentation was very well attended and several new aspects of the cases came out, but nothing about the footprint surfaced. We even enlisted the Van Meter librarians, Jolena Welker and Vickie Benson for more help, and asked them to reach out to their extensive contact list of Van Meter residents hoping that someone would be able to solve the mystery. As of today, no clue to the whereabouts of the footprint has been found. However, several experts at the Iowa Historical Society stated that our search for the footprint may all be for naught, as they expressed doubt that a plaster cast from 1903 would have been able to survive such a long period of years. Their reasoning was that the plaster used in 1903 would most likely have been relatively soft and brittle, and unless it was properly stored (like in a museum) the odds of it not crumbling to pieces decades ago were very slim. After all our research, the mystery of the strange footprint continues to live on, and out of all the possibilities, we like to hope that somewhere the footprint is still tucked away safely under a pile of dust in someone's attic or basement just waiting to be re-discovered.

15
Early Encounters:
Thunderbirds or Thoughtforms?
by Kevin Lee Nelson

Beings of Thunder and Light

As strange as the Van Meter incident was, it fits a pattern. Tales of large, winged creatures are found in indigenous oral traditions throughout the Upper Midwest going back centuries. The Ioway tribe lived in the south central part of Iowa where Van Meter is today. The Dakota Sioux had lands to the north and the Illini lived to the east near the Mississippi. According to Ioway oral traditions and archaeological findings, their tribe is descended from a much larger united tribe called the Oneota who lived in the area over a thousand years ago. The Oneota were the northern part of the Mississippian culture, also known as the "Mound Builders," which has been traced back to 800 C.E. Sadly, most of Iowa's indigenous people were forced out of the region in the early 1800s at the beginning of the Western Expansion. By the 1830s most had been relocated to reservations in Kansas and Oklahoma.

Many Northern Plains tribes had oral traditions mentioning unusual, winged creatures. The Ioway have a tale involving two of their most famous heroes, the mythical twins Dore and Wahredua. In the story, Dore and Wahredua climb a tall tree and encounter four winged men: Kho'-manyi (Thunder-man), Ukrimanyi (Lightning-man), I'yomani (Rain-man), and Wakandaiinye (Little-god). Each had magical powers to call up wind, rain, or thunder with their wings. Ukrimanyi had the power to shoot lightning from his eyes. However, even with these tremendous powers, they were outsmarted by the clever twins.

Tales of large, winged creatures called "Thunderbirds" are common among the Northern Plains tribes. The Lakota-Sioux call them "wakya," meaning "sacred winged-one." The Ojibwe (aka Chippewa) have a similar word for Thunderbirds, "wakinyan." They also use the word "animikeek," meaning "Thunderers." Indigenous people believed it was the Thunderbirds who created thunderstorms, particularly in the spring. Thunderbirds were thought to be benefic spirits if treated with respect. However, if angered, they could create destructive "wassmowin," the Ojibwe word for lightning. It is derived from the word "waskoneg," meaning "to give off light." According to Professor Theresa S. Smith, author of *The Island of Anishnaabeg: Thunderers and Water Monsters in the Traditional Ojibwe Life-World* (1995), "The Animikeek are often said to cause the sound of thunder by moving their huge wings and the flash of lightning by opening and closing their eyes." Other traditions say Thunderers are armed with a mighty bow and flaming arrows.

Thunderbirds are usually described as colossal birds...sometimes as big an airplane. In other traditions, like the Ioway tale, they are described as winged humanoids. Ojibwe elder William Trudeau described a Thunderbird, stating, "It looked something like a bird and it looked something like a man in places, like his legs, you know, and part of his body, but the face is something like a bird's face with a beak and wings on the sides."

Thunderbirds are also believed to communicate through their thunder. Smith writes, "While the speech of animikeek is not always clear it is intelligible, or at the very least potentially intelligible. And humans may exhibit their own powers to translate what is said. ... most agreed that something, usually a warning of some kind, was communicated." In *The Mothman Prophesies*, John Keel alludes to Thunderbird communication saying, "North American Indians have extensive legends about the Thunderbird, a huge bird said to carry off children and old people. It was accompanied by loud noises, hums, buzzes and, apparently, rumbles from the infrasonic and ultrasonic levels."

It is interesting how traditional descriptions of Thunderbirds parallel the Van Meter Visitor incident. Thunderbird traditions include large birds, sometimes described as humanoid beings with strange speech, and that are known to shine (or shoot) light. The latter resembles the mysterious projectiles or "magic arrows," a common theme in ultraterrestrial reports and folklore from aliens to fairies.

Like all good legends, powerful forces of good require a suitable nemesis. Thunderbirds are continually at war with their ancient enemies, which are often described as water monsters living deep within the lakes and rivers. Most prominent of these is Mishebeshu, meaning Great Lynx. The term Mishebeshu (also Mishepishu, Michipeshu, Mishibijiw, etc.) refers to breeds of malevolent, aquatic, feline entities, and it is also the name of their ruler. In many ways the creature(s) serve a similar role or are comparable to the Leviathan or Kraken in European mythology—a creature symbolizing darkness, cold, and the deeps...a being of the underworld. In contrast, the Thunderbird represents, light, heat, and the sky. They live in the liminal space between this world and the next and are mediators between man and the Great Spirit.

Indigenous lore is filled with stories of winged monsters. The Mi'kmaq have tales of a giant bird called the "Culloo" which was said to be a man-eater and was known to carry away children in its talons. The Apache tell stories about the "Owl-Man" or "Big Owl." He is man-sized, monstrous and used as a "bogeyman" to frighten children. The Penobscot tribe's legends include the dreaded "Pamola" (also Pomola, or Pamolai), a creature described as having the body of a man, the antlered head of a moose, and the wings and talons of an eagle. The mountains are sacred to Pamola, particularly Mt. Katadin in Maine. The "Moose of the Mountain" is still feared by some eastern tribes to this day. Like the Thunderbird, Pamola is said to control thunder and cause disastrous storms. In 1846, Henry David Thoreau mentioned Pamola. He writes:

> The tops of mountains are among the unfinished parts
> of the globe, whither it is a slight insult to the gods to
> climb and pry into their secrets, and try their effect on
> our humanity. Only daring and insolent men, perchance,
> go there. ... Pomola is always angry with those who
> climb to the summit of Ktaadn [sic].

The Terror on the Bluff

Many readers living the Midwest may be familiar with an old legend about a winged monster called the "Piasa" or "Piasa Bird." There is an enormous painting of the beast on a rock wall overlooking the Mississippi just outside Alton, Il. The name allegedly comes from an Illini word meaning "the bird that devours men." It is described as a dragon-like creature with horns and wings of a bat. According to legend, the Illini believed that it lived in the caves along the Mississippi River. The Piasa Bird would occasionally venture out of its lair, attack local villages, and carry off its victims to dine upon later. Finally it was killed by tribal warriors when it tried to attack Chief Ouatoga. Legend states the rock painting was made to commemorate the creature's demise.

Natives at Piasa Rock

It's a colorful story and well known to many. Unfortunately, it is false. It wasn't an intentional hoax, but rather an example of a tall tale taken too literally. In the essay "More 'Dinosaur' and 'Pterosaur' Rock Art That Isn't" published in *Palaeontologia Electronica* (2012), Phil Senter writes, "The alleged Illini legend and the character Ouatoga are the inventions of American author John Russell. Russell created this fake Illini legend and published it in *The Family Magazine* in 1836 and again in *Evangelical Magazine* and *Gospel Advocate* in 1848." But like all good yarns it contained a kernel of truth; the story was inspired by actual rock paintings. Senter adds that, according to Russell's son, he invented the story by adding his own imagination to a historic account of rock art discovered and documented by Father Marquette. When Father Jacques Marquette and Louis Joliet first saw the painting in 1673 Marquette wrote:

> As we coasted along the rocks, frightful for their height and length, we saw two monsters painted on these rocks, which startled us at first, and on which the boldest Indian dare not gaze long. They are as large as a calf, with horns on the head like a deer, a frightful look, red eyes, bearded like a tiger, the face somewhat like a man's, the body covered with scales, and a tail so long that it twice makes a turn of the body, passing over the head and down between the legs, and ending at last in a fish's tail. Green, red, and a kind of black are the colors employed.

Senter points out, "Marquette mentioned neither wings, nor the name Piasa, nor any legend or information that anyone provided about the paintings." The original paintings were likely of a type of water lynx or representation of Mishebeshu.

In the years following Marquette's report, local tribes were known to shoot at the formidable painting when passing by, perhaps as a way of showing their bravery. The painting became severely damaged over the years as a result. According to Canadian missionary J. F. Buisson de Saint-Cosme, most of the painting was destroyed by 1698 leaving only a vague outline of its former shape. In 1887, Russell commissioned an engraver to recreate the creature based on what remained of the rock painting (though the engraver never actually saw the surviving traces). The result was the popular (winged) depiction of the so-called Piasa Bird that remains to this day, though it scarcely resembles Marquette's description.

Artist Depiction of Piasa Bird

Residual Thoughtforms and Tulpas

Is it possible that ancient indigenous beliefs could have lasting effects today? Could mysterious winged beings be the result of residual psychic imprints from the past? Many of us are familiar with tall-tales of so-called "Indian curses" that last for generations or that are triggered by an act of desecration long after caster's death. Belief can be a powerful thing. There is a theory that asserts that powerful belief and emotions, altered states of consciousness, and prolonged focused concentration may actually *create* some of the otherworldly beings and anomalous effects people have experienced over the centuries. Strange manifestations and reports of unexplained phenomena have historically been linked to intense religious experiences, trance states, occult ritual, and powerful psychodrama.

An example of the latter would be a commonly reported experience involving an Ouija board. Typically when one uses an Ouija board, or "talking board," one is already in a heightened emotional state, usually a mixture of fear, apprehension, and excitement. Those using the board may be skeptical of whether or not it really works, but there is usually a part of them that wants to believe. Suddenly the board's planchette begins to move and spell out words that have personal significance to the participants. Each user assumes it is another participant who is moving the planchette and creating the ghostly messages. They may also hear knockings or experience other paranormal phenomena. Participants may assume they've contacted a ghost, but what they've likely done is project their own unconscious emotions and desires into their immediate environment and unintentionally created messages, effects, or even manifestations *themselves*. Ghost or not, it's still a very strange experience. This is an example of the "Thoughtform Theory," a.k.a. the "Tulpa Theory." The word "tulpa" is a Tibetan word meaning "to make" or "to construct" found in the *Tibetan Book of the Dead*.

A famous and well documented example of a thoughtform, or tulpa, was "The Philip Experiment" conducted in 1972 by a group of parapsychologists in Toronto. The researchers theorized they could "create a ghost" in a lab. A group of eight individuals invented an entire life history based around a fictitious person they called Philip Aylesford. They even mapped out his personality and created a portrait of what he looked like when alive. The group met for over a year to discuss Philip and make him as real as possible. Next they tried to make contact with their fictitious character though a séance. At first nothing happened, but eventually they experienced ghostly knocks and were given yes/no responses. As the participant's skepticism waned, Philip's messages became more detailed and physical phenomena increased. On one occasion he was believed to be responsible for making a table move from side to side and dance on one leg.

As astounding as this may sound, there were some questions that Philip could not answer. When asked questions to which none of the participants could possibly know the answer, Philip was unable to provide valid information. For example, when asked specific questions about 17th century life (the invented era in which Philip lived), he could not supply accurate answers. Researchers came to the conclusion that Philip was a manifestation created by (and comprised of) the collective thoughts of the group. Therefore, his knowledge was limited to that of the group members. This phenomenon is sometimes referred to as an "egregore," which stems from a Greek word *egeiro*, meaning "to raise up," "awaken," or "watch over." An egregore is created by a group of people engaged in focused group-mind activity. Their collective thoughts harmonize to create an entity that is representative of the group's beliefs, ideas, and goals. Most large corporations have created company egregores through corporate culture and brand identity which literally serve as "corporate entities." When an egregore seems to show independence, initiative, or take on a life of its own, it becomes a thoughtform or tulpa.

One could look at the tulpa phenomenon as an ancient form of artificial intelligence. While artificial intelligence, or A.I., is normally associated with robots and super-computers, it may be useful to look at tulpas as an ancient technology similar to our computer programs…psychic software, if you will. They have pre-programmed functions and features that originate with their creators. It is believed, like some types of software, that some tulpas can be extremely robust and outlast their creators. This may be the case with tulpas created by early indigenous populations. Perhaps belief in beings, like Thunderbirds, was so strong among certain tribes that they created thoughtforms which materialized into their reality in the shape of large, bird-like creatures. Maybe they *still* do.

It is also interesting that a large number of unexplained phenomena and cryptid sightings occur near burial mounds and sacred sites. In *The Beast of Bray Road: Trailing Wisconsin's Werewolf*, author Linda Godfrey writes of an incident that occurred outside Jefferson, WI in 1936. A night watchman spotted a tall, hairy, werewolf-like creature crouching and scratching at the earth atop an ancient burial mound. He encountered the creature on two separate nights and said it was accompanied by a powerful odor. Godfrey also noticed that a number of human-shaped effigy mounds throughout Wisconsin appear to have large pointed ears or horns. Perhaps the mounds represent wolfmen protector spirits.

Northeastern Iowa has a large number of mounds. Over two hundred of them are located at the Effigy Mound National Monument outside Harper's Ferry. Unfortunately, most of the mounds that existed throughout the Upper Midwest were destroyed by farming during the 19th century.

There is reason to believe mounds serve a dual purpose. Besides being used for burial, they may also be indicators of liminal areas, as mentioned in an earlier chapter. It is possible that certain entities were specifically created to be associated with sacred sites, serving as sentinels or guardian spirits. Like computer programs, they may remain "running in the background" and on stand-by for centuries after their creator's death. Eventually, they may be awakened through direct evocation or activated like spiritual golems to protect sacred tribal lands from acts of desecration. Perhaps they are somehow encoded or imprinted into the environment, like grooves in a record that replay when specific pre-programmed conditions are met. Whatever those conditions may be, they may have been triggered in Van Meter in the fall of 1903. The townspeople had a rare opportunity to witness something truly extraordinary, and they may have interacted with the mental creations of long-dead shamans.

FINAL
THOUGHTS

16
Reflections
by Noah Voss

The people who know a bit about what I do, will sporadically have questions about my latest project. A question I repeatedly fielded while speaking about this book was, "is there anything unusual happening there now?" In short, yes. We have all been back through the Van Meter area of Iowa multiple times researching, and investigating the 1903 case. We have also presented our findings to public audiences before the book was finished with hopes that we would uncover a new clue or more pieces to the story. Through all of this I personally have been approached by several people speaking about other oddities they've experienced. There were several unusual sightings reported to me including Bigfoot sightings. One such incident happened in front of a car in the clear illumination of headlights. Many folks shared a few reoccurring ghost stories. These hauntings were told of several different locations in Van Meter and then told to me again in the same vein by others. Perhaps this can be used to illustrate a larger paranormal oddity taking place in and around Van Meter. Most places I pass through have their folklore of a ghost or maybe a weird something someone's friend maybe once saw. What Van Meter has revealed to me so far seems to be a bit more unusual than the usual.

It is easy to brush aside such reports of the unexplained. Each of us has our to-do lists that we dutifully attack as our will and other dwindling resources allow. Such experiences whispered in the corner of crowded rooms are often less priority for most than when the next pay check arrives or that growing pile of laundry calling your name. Many people just don't have the option to focus on such things that are viewed to be aside to everything else that must get done. I understand and I myself am no stranger to losing sight of hope in the haze of stress.

I seem to find hope more often when I don't seek it directly. Rather I seem to find it on the other side of discovery that reveals intrigue and mystery. I believe myself fortunate that my voyages through dark and often dodgy parts pay me back many times in enigmatically obscure legends. There are so many truly unexplained events being continually experienced by those I speak with that I should think we will never run out of things to explore and bring back to you in our written word. This is at times the only wonderment I can find when I raise my eyes from the focus of a task to peer through the reality of the masses. It is easy to become bogged down by banter created to fulfill only the coffers of the few at the detriment of the many. Hope for me is found in the better educated than myself exploring the edge of reason with science and imagination. Many of whom seek knowledge for personal enlightenment while making their truly revolutionary findings available for others to consume. Hope for me is found in the welcoming people of Van Meter. Despite my own, often times unavoidably overt, ideas that disrupt common belief systems when gleaned by the observant outsider, the townsfolk of Van Meter have been outwardly nonjudgmental with kind eyes, curious questions and sincere smiles. There was no hiding the unusual motivation for me being in Van Meter and still they remained open to my research. I can count on one hand such a positive and embracing response despite my extensive travels over two decades, several countries and nearly all of the 50 states.

Van Meter may be at a crossroads regarding its unique past and how it decides to handle it into the future. Fighting against your own history is like battling a mountain you're trying to climb. You will more often be additionally successful if you figure out how to adapt to the mountain's environment. By utilizing the ideal routes on the Mountain, during the safer times of the day and night you increase your chances of success. This is one way I've come back from many a climbing expedition when others in footsteps very near my own have not. Professional mountaineers often voice; find a way to work with the mountain, not against it. I personally find many connections to purported paranormal hot spots and how the nearby communities respond. Countless times I've researched places that have plunked down fences, restricted hours, nailed up no-trespassing signs and pay for their local policing departments to patrol and ticket those who wander too close with curiosity. Of the few places that have embraced their new environments, I have viewed only wild successes.

Trying to control by restriction, and receiving instinctive push back from those inquisitive minds, one creates a naturally negative environment. Neglecting peoples positive attempts to gleam knowledge 'first hand' often times nurtures a dangerous set of conditions in these isolated locations. Others that embrace and package their history have regularly done so with great reward. By putting in the same effort as the alternative one can accomplish offering tours instead of tickets. It can cost less to present trash

bins and a light as opposed to fences with locked gates. Hanging inform-
ative placards that preserve the accurate history, instead of posting no-trespassing signs can change the unconscious impressions; from thoughts of
rebelling to that of learning through exploration. Van Meter, of course,
doesn't necessarily have one clear epicenter to "defend" or "cultivate."
The entire town has a uniquely fantastic history of events woven through
it. This presents the best opportunity in my mind, something the entire
town can get behind. To whatever extent the individual person or estab-
lishment feels comfortable, there is something for everyone from Van
Meter to embrace.

Narrowing positive efforts to a community focused event presents more
than a few opportunities during Visitor Days. Basically, an annual festival
themed around their unique history. Personally, I've always thought that
themes make a party. This would be a great excuse for the townsfolk and
other "visitors" to enjoy each other's company. I've lived in towns as small
as 4,000 and this kind of festival can easily be done and with no budget.
It just takes one motivated individual to get things started. With a little
luck, you'll be able to create a little agreement between those in charge.
Then get to work, and it's not that much the first year.

Set out some sawhorses on each end of the Main Street cordoning off the
block and you've got your location.

Van Meter Welcome Sign

There is always a group of kids nearby trying to get their band off the ground that would happily play for the exposure. Maybe a group of retirees that plays music together to get out of the house. Either way you've got your entertainment. Every small town has a bar and would usually jump at the opportunity to fire up a beer tent, and now you've got your entertainment for the over 21 crowd. I'd swing back through for the signature drink alone, the Visitor's Shadow (don't tell the tourists it's just a Black Russian garnished with a black licorice stick). Heck even the local Lions Club or the like would appreciate the chance to grill up some burgers and brats at their own expense to raise funds for their endeavors. That is a great first year for the Annual Visitor Days in Van Meter, Iowa.

Voss searches forests surrounding Van Meter Iowa for signs of ultraterrestrials

Even the late September anniversary of the creature sightings works well with the weather and segues stylishly into the Halloween season. The options are endless for engaging the residents. The Van Meter Visitor's Chase can loop through the town with folks jogging or walking for a small fee that helps to raise money for any worthy town expense. The Van Meter High School can hold a contest for its students to design the "official" shirt each year and the proceeds can go to raise funds for the library or some local need different every year. Before you know it, the town draws in venders willing to pay to set up their small booth for the arts and crafts fair. The possibilities only limited by the motivation and imagination of the people powering the event. This all can be as extravagant or relaxed as they feel comfortable with.

This does create a great opportunity to draw in tourists. Of course, it's nothing to be ashamed of but with sightseers does come their dollars and a lot of good for the community. The more tourists there are, the better the local businesses do. This allows them to expand and offer more convenient services to, not only the occasional traveler, but to the residents year round. The more tourist dollars that come in, the more taxes are carried by non-residents and eventually less tax money is needed from the residents. It is good to have choices and clearly Van Meter has many to choose from. Having choices can be a supremely exciting place to be.

I happily wonder how many more places right here in America might have their own odd and unexplained events in their history, as of yet undocumented by outsiders. Despite how I am greeted or treated when I show up, I have hope. Where will our adventures take us next? Wherever we land, whatever story we dig up in the future, I hope you find the written account of our exploration worthy of your time.

17
The Van Meter Mystery As I See It
by Chad Lewis

I can honestly say that after poring over countless records, interviewing residents, unearthing local history and touring the sites of the original encounters, I am still as puzzled today as the people of Van Meter were back in 1903. When I first began researching this case I was convinced that it would turn out to be nothing more than some sort of twisted hoax, yet as I made my way through months of research, the idea of the monster being some sort of prank or joke quickly eroded away. If there is conclusive evidence of a hoax out there, we were unable to find it. Next, my theory turned to the idea that perhaps the miners had inadvertently unleashed a previously unknown beast that had been hidden safely beneath the surface of the earth for who knows how long. This theory also fell apart due to the creature exhibiting powers that no known creature of earth possesses (impervious to weapons, super human movement, memory erasing odors, etc.). I also tossed out the idea that all of these prominent townspeople simply got confused and mistook a large pelican for a giant, eight-foot-tall bat like creature. The problem was that no sooner had I constructed one explanation, when new evidence pushed it right back down and I was forced to start over once again. When all the dust was settled, I had acquired more questions than answers.

Lewis searching downtown Van Meter for the Visitor

Finding oneself in the midst of complete puzzlement is not the ideal position for someone setting out to solve a mystery, yet that is exactly where I am now squarely situated. In today's world where we crave answers for everything and increasingly disregard gray areas in pursuit of black and white certainties, the space for mystery and the unexplained is perpetually shrinking. I have found peace in knowing that I may never discover what happened in Van Meter during that fateful week of 1903, and perhaps I am not meant to. Perhaps the answer is not nearly as important as the act of seeking it out.

18
Van Meter's Enduring Enigma
by Kevin Lee Nelson

In our research, my co-authors and I often encounter strange, but familiar, stories that are widespread from state to state. Most people do not realize how ubiquitous they are, as the names and locations are often changed to reflect one's area or add local color, but the stories remains essentially the same. Perhaps the most prevalent of these is the classic "Vanishing Hitch-hiker" tale. Every region has its own variant of this urban legend, often changing over time like the "telephone game". Such tales are an important part of the fabric of American folklore because they tend to reflect our cultural values, beliefs, and fears. Interestingly, through spooky stories we may learn far more about *ourselves* than about paranormal phenomena. For example, one of the first reactions to the "Vanishing Hitchhiker" story that one hears today is, "Why did they pick up a hitchhiker? Don't they know that's dangerous?" This was not a common belief just a couple generations ago, and it reflects prevailing feelings of anxiety and distrust within our society. However, not all tales follow familiar patterns, or necessarily have something to teach; sometimes unexplainable things just happen.

When we first began researching the Van Meter Visitor case we immediately recognized it was something unique. This was not just another alleged haunting, Bigfoot sighting, or alien abduction claim; it was an incident that was truly bizarre, well documented, and unlike any we'd encountered before... or so we thought. You see, only later, after analyzing the events and examining the characteristics of the mysterious Visitor, did we begin to realize that the incident could be part of a much larger, ongoing, and perhaps ancient, phenomena. We began to see common threads between this case and others, particularly the Mothman incidents of 1966-'67.

What made the Van Meter case so exciting is that it occurred a sixty years *before* Mothman. And like the Mothman, the Van Meter Visitor defies explanation. It also occurred six years *before* the rash of "Jersey Devil" sightings in 1909, removing the possibility that witnesses were influenced by news reports describing a "strange winged creature" with "glowing eyes" and a "high-pitched scream." This makes Van Meter a very interesting case because it predates the rest, thus lending validity. One could even consider the Van Meter Visitor a proto-Mothman case. Furthermore, unlike most anomalous cases, there isn't a single explanation that far outweighs the rest; all the potential explanations have their own strengths and drawbacks. As such, the case defies "Occam's Razor," a principle that state's "the simplest answer is usually the correct one", because there is no simple answer. This is why we have explored a number of avenues, from the mundane hoax to exotic theories about ultraterrestrials. In the end, it is up to the reader to decide. However, we also acknowledge that in our attempt to shed light on this mystery may have only created *more* mystery. Thus, after careful examination with no clear-cut answers, we are left with one thing: an enduring enigma. This, I believe, is the best possible outcome.

Nelson researching the site of the old brick factory

If we discovered the creature was a surviving specimen of a now-extinct species, the story would be over, much like that of the Dodo bird or Tasmanian tiger. Had it proven to be a hoax it would have been a bittersweet accomplishment, having replaced a great campfire tale with an unfortunate, and far less interesting, bit of chicanery. Instead, we're left scratching our heads with more questions than answers; the mystery remains unsolved. Even so, I feel it is a positive outcome because it ensures that future generations will look back and wonder, *"What was it that visited Van Meter?"*

19
Van Meter Today
by Chad Lewis

To the casual observer, little about Van Meter has changed over the past 100 years. Granted, the progress of technology is clearly visible everywhere, but the pace of life still harkens back to a simpler time, residents continue to greet one another by name, and a lively sense of community still thrives among townsfolk. So far the people of Van Meter have rebuked Des Moines' flirtatious advances, even as the "big city" continues to gobble up land on its pursuit west towards town. One day, Des Moines will likely overtake Van Meter, but for now residents take great pride in being somewhat removed from big city life. After nearly 110 years, the population of Van meter is practically the same as it was in 1903, when approximately 1,000 people called the town home. Contrary to the theory of out of control urbanization, if anything, the downtown of Van Meter has shrunk in size over time. Gone are the days of multiple saloons, general mercantiles, grocers, butchers, blacksmiths and milliners. Today, the easily navigated two block section of downtown is comprised of a requisite Post Office, a friendly bar and grill, a rustic auto part shop, City Hall, the Fire Department, and a wonderful public library.

Downtown Van Meter

In today's hurried world, the majority of cruising vehicles along Interstate 80 are not willing to deviate from their predetermined directions in order to trek an additional two miles to Van Meter just to check it out. This has somewhat insulated Van Meter from the accidental tourists enjoyed by other towns not bypassed by the Interstate. With this Interstate created isolation, the tourist frenzy that accompanies many other towns that feature a paranormal legend simply sidestepped Van Meter. If you are hoping to stick your face in the cutout of a giant wooden bat-like creature for a photo remembrance, or marvel at the large town mural of the bizarre creature emerging from the old mine, you will be sorely disappointed. You can't find bumper stickers claiming "Come Visit the Van Meter Visitor" (trademark pending), coal mine key chains, eerie postcards, T-shirts with attached bat wings, or any of the other wide assortment of tourist memorabilia that is readily available in other paranormal hotspots. As of today, any indication of the Van Meter Visitor is all but absent from the town, although I believe (and hope) that this will soon change as a growing portion of the population is looking to embrace its strange monster history. Sometimes local history just needs some time to marinate among the locals before they are ready to serve it up to the greater general public.

Appendix A
Businesses Operating in Van Meter During 1903
by Chad Lewis

Here a few of the Van Meter businesses that were in operation during the 1903 encounter.

L.F. Moore Restaurant – Mr. Moore operated a restaurant that also stocked canned goods, candles, cigars, fruits, and an assortment of fresh baked cakes and pies. In a Des Moines advertisement, Mr. Moore touted his light drinks, ice cream, and fresh oysters (in season).

Van Schaack's Meat Market – Operated by Messrs. J.C. & V.H. Van Schaack. Customers were guaranteed of fresh meat as the firm did all of their own killing and rendering.

Sweezy's Meat Market – C.H. Sweezy, Proprietor. First opened in 1892, the market was known for being well-stocked. All livestock killing was also done onsite.

Riverview Farm – Operated by W.A. Jones. The Riverview Farm was widely known throughout the state for its high quility hogs.

Van Meter Drug Store – Operated by Dr. N.P. Summers, an old time practitioner. It was located just south of the hotel. In addition to carrying drugs, the store also sold toys, perfumes, and holiday goods.

Van Meter State Bank – Owned by the Goar brothers, the bank was operated by Clarence (Peter) Dunn, who also happened to be a main witness to the Van Meter Visitor. We have no word of how much it cost to replace the bank window that Mr. Dunn shot out.

Dentist – Dr. J.H. Dwight was located in an office building one block west of the Van Meter flour mill. To lure in fearful customers, Dr. Dwight advertised a "painless extraction method."

Photographer – C.W. Smith. – Smith's gallery was located on Main Street, just west of the post office. Mr. Smith was said to have taken photos of nearly everybody in and around Van Meter.

G.R. Pugh's Barber Shop – Owned by G.R. Pugh. The barber shop was located just south of the post office. Pugh claimed to specialize in the latest styles of hair dressing.

Griffith Brothers Implement – Owned by brothers U.G. and David Griffith. – By all accounts, the Griffith brothers ran a well-respected and profitable implement store. We are unsure as to the location of the business.

Manbeck's General Store – Owned by George E. Manbeck. The general store was a big brick building on the southwest corner of town with big glass windows that showcased its neatly decorated stock. Manbeck's seemed to have everything a person could want with shoes, canned goods, clothing, glassware, bedding, and much more.

O.V. White's Hardware – O.V. White, proprietor – A photos of Mr. White's store is on the cover of this book and the side wall of the building advertises hardware, furniture, and carpets.

Post Office – The postmaster of the office was H.H. Phillips who was the author of the original article on the strange creature. We can assume that the post office had all the services of an average post office of the time.

Platt Pressed Brick Company – Operated by several generations of the Pratt family the brick and coal mine company was praised for its superior products. The mine was closed down after a strike.

Van Meter Flour Mill – Operated by J.R. Van Meter. In 1901, to help facilitate the projected growth of the mill, the town donated the sum of $2,660.

**Other Van Meter Businesses that we know little about:

Van Meter Hotel – Mentioned briefly in a few articles, we have found no specifics on the business. We believe that it was operated by Charles McCoy.

Dr. Alcott's Office – Based on the *Des Moines Daily News* article, Dr. Alcott had a sleeping area above his office somewhere downtown.

Sidney Gregg's Store – The *Des Moines Daily News* article mentioned that Mr. Gregg was sleeping inside his store which was said to be located just around the corner from O.V. White's Hardware Store.

Saloons – Unfortunately little is known about the various saloons in Van Meter. Thanks to the Van Meter Centennial History book, we at least know the names of the saloon operators as L.F. Arnold, Roy Lloyd, Dale McNair, Ernie Strunk, Stankey. Schultz, D. Mapes, Ethel Smith, and Ethel Logan.

Mather & Gregg's building – We are uncertain what businesses were inside this building. However, based on the *Des Moines Daily News* article Sidney Gregg was said to be sleeping in his store when the creature appeared. The specifics of Gregg's store is unknown.

Appendix B
Read All About It: The Original Newspaper Accounts

Dealing with newspaper articles from the late 1800s and early 1900s is a tricky business rife with catchy but misleading headlines, severe embellishments, and even a few outright hoaxes. Perhaps a "Half human - half centipede" was actually born in Texas during 1884 as reported by the *Galveston Daily News*. Or perhaps it was just a really slow news day in the press room and an imaginative reporter dreamed up the story to make his deadline. Many U.S. cities had several competing newspapers, and in such a cut-throat business, it was common practice for some newspaper men to suspend the truth in order to increase their sales. Having written several books focusing on peculiar newspaper stories of the early 1900s, I have researched all types of strange and seemingly unbelievable stories. And while it is true that some of the stories of the time period turned out to be pure fiction, I have discovered that the vast majority of articles, regardless of how outlandish they initially sounded, usually contained mostly truths. For instance, when a giant sword fish (a saltwater fish) was said to have been caught in a small secluded Wisconsin river (freshwater), the fisherman sensed the skepticism that awaited him and decided to lug the still flopping fish down to the local newspaper's offices to prove his story. The misplaced fish was exhibited at the newspaper for all disbelievers to behold. Instead of outlandish hoaxes coming from respected local journalists, what I found was a penchant among editors to create the most eye-catching headlines, which in turn would generate the most sales. It was all too common to read headlines like: Made Insane By Ghosts, Cows Bark Like Dogs, Chicken Has Human Face, and Foretold His Own Death to grace the covers of daily papers.

The sensational story of the Van Meter incident quickly spread through newspapers around the country. The encounter was first reported by H.H. Phillips in the October 4th edition of the *Des Moines Daily News*. The very next day the *Des Moines Daily News* printed a follow up story which warned that the original article may have been exaggerated, but gave no specifics. From here the trajectory of the story takes an odd turn as the *New York World* publishes a version of the story that contained two glowing errors: 1. They changed O.V. White to Dr. O.V. White, although he was a hardware store owner. 2. The paper changed the spelling of Dr. Alcott to "Olcott." These two errors would end up getting repeated in nearly every subsequent article. One day after the *New York World* published their mistake ridden article, the *Des Moines Daily Capitol* looked to embarrass their rival Des Moines paper by releasing a very skeptical article changeling the veracity of the Van meter events. Soon the story was picked up by several dozen newspapers from around the country. Most of the papers simply re-printed one of several stock articles that told the full story of the encounters. Rather than list 20 copies of the same story, we have only included the articles that differ from one another. All the articles are listed below:

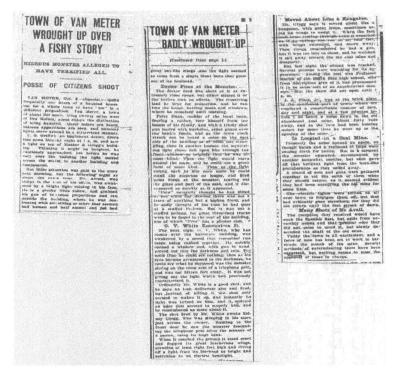

Town of Van Meter Wrought Up Over a Fishy Story
Hideous Monster Alleged to Have Terrified All
Posse of Citizens Shoot

Van Meter- Oct 3 (Special) – Quite frequently one hears of a haunted house, but for a whole town to have 'em' is a different proposition. Van Meter, a town of about 900 souls, lying 20 miles west of Des Moines, alone enjoys the distinction of being haunted. Queer noises are heard, hideous apparitions are seen and uncanny lights move around in a mysterious manner.

U.G. Griffith an implement dealer, drove into town Monday night at 1 a.m. and saw a light on top of Mather & Gregg's building. Thinking it might be buglers, he cautiously approached, but before he was very near the building the light moved across the street to another building and disappeared.

But little attention was paid to the story next morning, but the following night at about the same hour Dr. Alcott, who sleeps in the rear of his office was awakened by a bright light shining in his face. He is a plucky little fellow, and grabbed his gun of immense proportions and ran outside the building, where he was confronted with something or other that seemed half human and half animal and yet had great bat-like wings, and the light seemed to come from a single blunt horn that grew out of its forehead.

Doctor Fires at the Monster

The doctor fired five shots at it at extremely close range, but either missed it or the bullets took no effects. The remaining load he kept for protection, and he ran into the house, barring dorrs and windows, where he remained until morning.

Peter Dunn, cashier of the local bank, fearing a robber, tore himself from the bosom of his family, and with a trusty shotgun loaded with buckshot, stood guard over the bank's funds, and as the town clock struck one he heard a noise of the eastside of the building as of someone strangling, then in another instant the mysterious light shone full upon him through the front window so brightly that he was almost blind. The the light would move around the room, and he could see a great form of some kind. Then as the light swung back to him once more he could stand the suspense no longer, and fired point blank at the monster, tearing out the glass and part of the sash, and it disappeared as quickly as it appeared. "Pete" naturally thought he had killed it, but when day dawned there was not a trace of anything but a broken front, and he sadly thought of the time he shot at a stuffed pelican. But this was not a stuffed pelican, for great three-toed tracks were to be found in the rear of the building, one of which "Pete" has a plaster cast.

O.V. White Encounters It

The next night O.V. White, who has rooms over the hardware building was awakened by a sound that resembled two rasps being rubbed together. He quickly opened a window and, with gun in hand, peered out into the darkness and rain. For some time he could see nothing, then as his eyes became accustomed to the darkness, he could see what he supposed was the monster sitting on the cross arm of a telephone pole, and was not fifteen feet away. It was not giving out the light which had previously characterized it.

Ordinarily Mr. White is a good shot, and he says he took deliberate aim and fired, but instead of killing it the shot only seemed to waken it up, and instantly its light was turned on him, and it emitted an odor that seemed to stupefy him, and he remembered no more about it. The shot fired by Mr. White awoke Sidney Gregg, who was sleeping in his store just across the corner. Rushing to the front door he saw the monster descending the telephone pole after the manner of a parrot, using its huge beak. When it reached the ground it stood erect and flapped its great featherless wings, standing at least eight feet high and giving off a light from its forehead as bright and searching as an electric headlight.

Moved About Like a Kangaroo

Mr. Gregg says it moved about like a kangaroo, with great leaps, sometimes using its wings to assist it. When the fast mail came tearing through town it crouched as if to spring, but ran on all four feet with wings extended, and sailed away. The Gregg remembered he had a gun, but it was too late to shoot, and he watched it sail away toward the old coal mine and disappear. But last night the climax was reached. Several persons were watching for its appearance. Among the rest was Professor Martin of the South Side High School, who from description gave of it had pronounced it to be some sort of an antediluvian monster. But the show did not open until 1 a.m.

J.L. Platt Jr., was at the brick plant in the northwest part of town, where are employed a considerably number of men day and night, and at a few minutes before 1 he heard a noise down in the old abandoned coal mine about forty rods away, and as the men had been hearing noises for some time he went up to the opening of the mine.

Is Located in a coal mine

Presently the noise opened up again, as though Satan and a regiment of imps were coming forth for battle. But in a moment the monster appeared, accompanied by another somewhat smaller, but each gave off that brilliant light from the horn-like protuberance as they sailed away. A crowd of men and guns were gathered together to rid the earth of them when they should return, as it seemed evident they had been occupying the old mine for some time. The electric lights were turned on all over town to frighten them off, but they had evidently gone elsewhere, for they did not return until the first streak of dawn.

Many Shots of No Avail

The reception they received would have sunk the Spanish fleet, but aside from unearthly noises and that peculiar odor they did not seem to mind it, but slowly descended the shaft of the old mine. Today the town is all excitement, and a force of men has been set to work to barricade the mouth of the mine. Several methods of exterminating them have been suggested, but nothing seems to meet the approval of those in charge.

Des Moines Daily News, October 4, 1903

Van Meter Hot Under the Collar
Town has been maligned by ghost stories
Citizens of the place feel indignant over the matter,
as it gives the places an unenviable reputation

The town of Van Meter is justly indignant over a series of articles that have appeared in the *Daily News* and the *Capitol* is in receipt of a number of letters from citizens of that place who feel highly indignant over the matter. The articles alleged that the town was highly wrought up over the alleged affair. The principal article started out with the following:

"Quite frequently one hears of a haunted house, but for a whole town to have 'em' is a different proposition. Van Meter, a town of about 900 souls, lying 20 miles west of Des Moines, alone enjoys the distinction of being haunted. Queer noises are heard, hideous apparitions are seen and uncanny lights move around in a mysterious manner."

In a letter received by the *Capital* it was stated "It is very apparent on the face of every sane person that it is pure fabrication, but to the residents of the town here it is the height of foolishness. It seems as though the corporation manufactured this story from an incident or two and sent it into the news. They published the yarn and then began to investigate its source. They sent several telephone calls to the central office here asking concerning the party and stating that he was the author of their rampant story. That is generally their way of doing business."

"A traveling man with Swift & Co. of your city was in town today and came around to see the ruins, but there was none in sight."

"Now we would like for you people to devote a little space to this attached article with the purpose in view of squaring us with the outside world and showing the policy of the *News* in first publishing such articles and then investigating the source."

Des Moines Daily Capitol, October 6, 1903

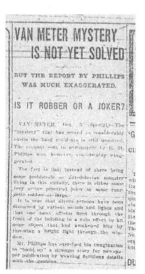

Van Meter Mystery Not Solved
But the report by Phillips was much exaggerated
Is it robber or a joker?

Van Meter, Oct. 5 - (Special) The "mystery" that has served to considerably excite the residents is still unsolved. The account sent to newspapers by H.H. Phillips was however, considerably exaggerated. The fact is that instead of there being some prehistoric or antediluvian monster living in this vicinity, there is either some very active practical joker or some energetic robber at large. It is true that divers persons have been disturbed by various sounds and lights and that one bank official fired through the front of the building in a vain effort to hit some object that had awakened him by throwing a bright light through the window. Mr. Phillips has exercised his imagination to "build up" a stronger story for newspaper publication by weaving fictitious details with the genuine.

Des Moines Daily News, October 5, 1903

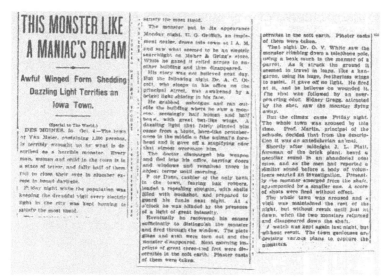

This Monster Like A Maniac's Dream
Awful Winged Form Shedding Dazzling Light Terrifies an Iowa Town

Des Moines, Ia., Oct 4 - The town of Van Meter, containing 1,000 persons is terribly wrought up by what is described as a horrible monster. Every man, woman, and child in the town is in a state of terror, and fully half of them fail to close their eyes in slumber except in broad daylight. Friday night while the population was keeping the dreadful vigil every electric light in the city was kept burning to satisfy the most timid. The monster put in its appearance Monday night, U.G. Griffith, an implement dealer, drove into town at 1 A.M. and saw what seemed to be an electric search-light on Maher & Grigg's store. While he gazed it sailed across to another building and then disappeared.

His story was not believed the next day. But the following night Dr. A.C. Olcott, who sleeps in his office on the principal street, was awakened by a bright light shining in his face. He grabbed a shotgun and ran outside the building where he saw a monster, seemingly half human and half beast, with great bat-like wings. A dazzling light that fairly blinded him came from a blunt, horn-like protuberance in the middle of the animal's fore-head, and it gave off a stupefying odor that almost overcame him. The doctor discharged his weapon and fled into his office, barring doors and windows, and remained there in abject terror until morning. Peter Dunn, cashier of the only bank in the town, fearing bank robbers, loaded a repeating shotgun with shells filled with buckshot and prepared to guard his funds next night. At 2 o'clock he was blinded by the presence of a light of great intensity.

Eventually he recovered his senses sufficiently to distinguish the monster and fired through the window. The plate glass and sash were torn out and the monster disappeared. Next morning imprints of great three-toed feet were distinguishable in the soft earth. Plaster casts of them were taken. That night Dr. O.V. White saw the monster climbing down a telephone pole, using a beak much in the manner of a parrot. As it struck the ground it seemed to travel in leaps, like a kangaroo, using its huge featherless wings to assist. It gave off no light. He fired at it, and he believes he wounded it. The shot was followed by an overpowering odor. Sidney Gregg, attracted by the shot saw the monster flying away.

But the climax came Friday night. The whole town was aroused by this time. Prof. Martin, principal of the schools, decided that upon the description it was an antediluvian animal. Shortly after midnight J.L. Platt, foreman of the brick plant, heard a peculiar sound in an abandoned coal mine, and as the men had reported a similar sound before a body of volunteers started an investigation. Presently the monster emerged from the shaft, accompanied by a smaller one. A score of shots were fired without effect. The whole town was aroused and a vigil was maintained the rest of the night, but without result, until just at dawn, when the two monsters returned and disappeared down the shaft. Watch was kept again last night, but without result. The town geniuses are devising various plans to capture the monsters.

New York World, October 5, 1903

That Winged Monster

From a town in Iowa comes the report that a horrible monster has appeared. This monster is said to be half human, half beast, with great bat-like wings and three-toed feet. The report further says that it is bulletproof and amuses itself by running up and down telephone poles. We learn, upon investigation, that the town from which the report comes is not a prohibition town. A few years ago some genius working in a quarry, cut an immense footprint in the rock with his chisel. The he informed the local newspaper of his "find" and in a short time scientific men from all over the world were visiting this remarkable quarry and offering strange opinions on this "antediluvian" relic. Such happenings afford excellent material for soliloquy. They are interesting things to dream about. But to think about, and think seriously, more matter-of-fact subjects are required. Business subjects, for instances. You will find plenty of good, serious thinking material in the The World's "Business Opportunities."

The New York Evening World, October 6, 1903

A Winged Monster
Creature Emitting a Dazzling Light Terrifies Hawkeyes

Des Moines, Iowa, Oct. 10 - The town of Van Meter, containing 1,000 persons is terribly wrought up by what is described as a horrible monster. Every man, woman, and child in the town is in a state of terror, and fully half of them fail to close their eyes in slumber except in broad daylight. The monster put in an appearance Monday night. U.G. Griffith, an implement dealer, drove into town at 1 a.m. and saw what seemed to be an electric searchlight on Maher & Grigg's store. While he gazed it sailed across to another building and then disappeared. His story was not believed the next day. But the following night Dr. A.C. Olcott, who sleeps in his office on the principal street, was awakened by a bright light shining in his face. He grabbed a shotgun and ran outside the building where he saw a monster, seemingly half human and half beast, with great bat-like wings. A dazzling light that fairly blinded him came from a blunt, horn-like protuberance in the middle of the animal's forehead, and it gave off a stupefying odor that almost overcame him. The doctor discharged his weapon and fled into his office, barring doors and windows, and remained there in abject terror until morning. Peter Dunn, cashier of the only bank in the town, fearing bank robbers, loaded a repeating shotgun with shells filled with buckshot and prepared to guard his funds next night. At about 2 o'clock he was blinded by the presence of a light of great intensity. Eventually he recovered his senses sufficiently to distinguish the monster and fired through the window. The plate glass and sash were torn out and the monster disappeared. Next morning imprints of great three-toed feet were distinguishable in the soft earth. Plaster casts of them were taken.

That night Dr. O.V. White saw the monster climbing down a telephone pole, using a beak much in the manner of a parrot. As it struck the ground it seemed to travel in leaps, like a kangaroo, using its huge featherless wings to assist. It gave off no light. He fired at it, and he believes he wounded it. The shot was followed by an overpowering odor. Sidney Gregg, attracted by the shot saw the monster flying away. But the climax came last night. The whole town was aroused by this time. Prof. Martin, principal of the schools, decided that upon the description it was an antediluvian animal. Shortly after midnight J.L. Platt, foreman of the brick plant, heard a peculiar sound in an abandoned coal mine, and as the men had reported a similar sound before a body of volunteers started an investigation. Presently the monster emerged from the shaft, accompanied by a smaller one. A score of shots were fired without effect. The whole town was aroused and vigil was maintained the rest of the night, but without result, until just at dawn, when the two monsters returned and disappeared down the shaft.

The Saint Paul Globe, October 11, 1903

Des Moines' New Monster
Citizens Tell Weird Tales of This Modern Terror

Des Moines- Oct. 12- According to prominent citizens, two weird-looking terror-stricken monsters are living in an abandoned coal mine on the edge of the town. At night they come out and act as sort of town curfew bell-everyone locks the doors and hides under beds or behind curtains. Residents whose veracity heretofore has been unquestioned tell harrowing stories of experiences with the horrible monsters. Dr. A.C. Olcott, awakened by a bright light shining through his window, says the terror he saw was half human and half beast, with great bat-like wings. A dazzling light that fairly blinded him came from a blunt horn-like protuberance in the middle of the animal's forehead, and it gave off a stupefying odor that almost overcame him.

Peter Dunn, cashier of the bank, fired his shotgun at the monster. Next morning imprints of great three-toed feet were discernible in the soft earth. Plaster casts of them were taken. Dr. O.V. White saw the monster climbing down a telephone pole, using a beak much in the manner of a parrot. As it struck the ground it seemed to travel in leaps, featherless wings to assist. It gave off no light. He fired at it. The shot was followed by an overpowering odor. Sidney Gregg attracted by the shot, saw the monster flying away. J.L. Platt, foreman of the brick plant, heard a peculiar sound in an abandoned coal mine. Presently the monster emerged from the shaft, accompanied by a smaller one. A sore of shots were fired without effect. The whole town was aroused and just at dawn the two monsters returned and disappeared down the shaft.

Waterloo Daily Courier, October 12, 1903

Create A Reign of Terror
Two Peculiar Monsters Said to Be at Large in Iowa

According to prominent Des Moines citizens, two weird-looking terror-stricken monsters are living in an abandoned coal mine on the edge of the town. At night they come out and act as sort of town curfew bell—everyone locks the doors and hides under beds or behind curtains. Residents whose veracity heretofore has been unquestioned tell harrowing stories of experiences with the horrible monsters. Dr. A.C. Olcott, awakened by a bright light shining through his window, says the terror he saw was half human and half beast, with great bat-like wings. A dazzling light that fairly blinded him came from a blunt horn-like protuberance in the middle of the animal's forehead, and it gave off a stupefying odor that almost overcame him.

Peter Dunn, cashier of the bank, fired his shotgun at the monster. Next morning imprints of great three-toed feet were discernible in the soft earth. Plaster casts of them were taken. Dr. O.V. White saw the monster climbing down a telephone pole, using a beak much in the manner of a parrot. As it struck the ground it seemed to travel in leaps, featherless wings to assist. It gave off no light. He fired at it. The shot was followed by an overpowering odor. Sidney Gregg attracted by the shot, saw the monster flying away. J.L. Platt, foreman of the brick plant, heard a peculiar sound in an abandoned coal mine. Presently the monster emerged from the shaft, accompanied by a smaller one. A sore of shots were fired without effect. The whole town was aroused and just at dawn the two monsters returned and disappeared down the shaft.

Emmetsburg Iowa Democrat, October 14, 1903

Dazzled An Iowa Town
Winged Monster Scared the Populace

The town of Van Meter, containing 1,000 persons is terribly wrought up by what is described as a horrible monster. Every man, woman and child in the town is in a state of terror, and fully half of them fail to close their eyes in slumber expect in broad daylight. The monster put in its appearance Monday night. U.G. Griffith, an implement dealer, drove into town at 1 a.m. and saw what seemed to be an electric searchlight on Maher & Grigg's store. While he gazed it sailed across to another building and then disappeared. His story was not believed the next day. But the following night Dr. A.C. Olcott, who sleeps in his office on the principal street, was awakened by a bright light shining in his face.

He grabbed a shotgun and ran outside the building where he saw a monster, seemingly half human and half beast, with great bat-like wings. A dazzling light that fairly blinded him came from a blunt, horn-like protuberance in the middle of the animal's forehead, and it gave off a stupefying odor that almost overcame him. The doctor discharged his weapon and fled into his office, barring doors and windows, and remained there in abject terror until morning. Peter Dunn, cashier of the only bank in the town, fearing bank robbers, loaded a repeating shotgun with shells filled with buckshot and prepared to guard his funds next night. At about 2 o'clock he was blinded by the presence of a light of great intensity. Eventually he recovered his senses sufficiently to distinguish the monster and fired through the window. The plate glass and sash were torn out and the monster disappeared. Next morning imprints of great three-toed feet were distinguishable in the soft earth. Plaster casts of them were taken.

That night Dr. O.V. White saw the monster climbing down a telephone pole, using a beak much in the manner of a parrot. As it struck the ground it seemed to travel in leaps, like a kangaroo, using its huge featherless wings to assist. It gave off no light. He fired at it, and he believes he wounded it. The shot was followed by an overpowering odor. Sidney Gregg, attracted by the shot saw the monster flying away. But the climax came Friday night. The whole town was aroused by this time. Prof. Martin, principal of the schools, decided that upon the description it was an antediluvian animal. Shortly after midnight J.L. Platt, foreman of the brick plant, heard a peculiar sound in an abandoned coal mine, and as the men had reported a similar sound before a body of volunteers started an investigation. Presently the monster emerged from the shaft, accompanied by a smaller one. A score of shots were fired without effect. The whole town was aroused and vigil was maintained the rest of the night, but without result, until just at dawn, when the two monsters returned and disappeared down the shaft.

Newport Hoosier State, November 18, 1903

Monster Of Awful Form
Horrible Winged Beast That Appeared in an Iowa Town

The town of Van Meter, Ia., containing 1,000 persons, is terribly wrought up by what is described as a horrible monster. The thing, whatever it is put on an appearance one night about three weeks ago. U.G. Griffith, an implement dealer, drove into town at 1 o'clock a.m. and saw what seemed to be an electric search light on Maher & Gregg's store. While he gazed it sailed across to another building and then disappeared. His story was not believed the next day. But the following night Dr. A.C. Olcott, who sleeps in his office on the principal street, was awakened by a bright light shining in his face. He grabbed a shotgun and ran outside the building where he saw a monster, seemingly half human and half beast, with great bat-like wings. A dazzling light that fairly blinded him came from a blunt, horn-like protuberance in the middle of the animal's forehead, and it gave off a stupefying odor that almost overcame him.

The doctor discharged his weapon and fled into his office, barring doors and windows, and remained there in abject terror until morning. Peter Dunn, cashier of the only bank in the town, fearing bank robbers, loaded a repeating shotgun with shells filled with buckshot and prepared to guard his funds next night. At about 2 o'clock he was blinded by the presence of a light of great intensity. Eventually he recovered his senses sufficiently to distinguish the monster and fired through the window. The plate glass and sash were torn out and the monster disappeared. Next morning imprints of great three-toed feet were distinguishable in the soft earth. Plaster casts of them were taken.

That night Dr. O.V. White saw the monster climbing down a telephone pole, using a beak much in the manner of a parrot. As it struck the ground it seemed to travel in leaps, like a kangaroo, using its huge featherless wings to assist. It gave off no light. He fired at it, and he believes he wounded it. The shot was followed by an overpowering odor. Sidney Gregg, attracted by the shot saw the monster flying away. But the climax came Friday night. The whole town was aroused by this time. Prof. Martin, principal of the schools, decided that upon the description it was an antediluvian animal. Shortly after midnight J.L. Platt, foreman of the brick plant, heard a peculiar sound in an abandoned coal mine, and as the men had reported a similar sound before a body of volunteers started an investigation. Presently the monster emerged from the shaft, accompanied by a smaller one. A score of shots were fired without effect. The whole town was aroused and vigil was maintained the rest of the night, but without result, until just at dawn, when the two monsters returned and disappeared down the shaft.

Eau Claire Daily Telegram, November 19, 1903

Bibliography

Chapter 1 - Unearthing a Legend
"Des Moines' New Monster." *Waterloo Daily Courier*, December 12, 1903.

Chapter 3 - Early History of Van Meter
Centennial Book Committee. *Van Meter Centennial History*. Van Meter, IA., 1970.

Chapter 3 - History of the Brick Factory and Mine
Iowa Geological Survey; Volume 8. 1898.
"J.L.Platt." *Humeston New Era*, February 8, 1893.
Wood, R.F. *Past and Present of Dallas County, Iowa*. Nabu Press. 2010.

Chapter 4 - Paranormal Beliefs of 1903 Van Meter
Flaherty, Ray. *Our Lizard creek Farm*. Vantage Press. 1969.
"Is it a Sea Serpent?" *Estherville Vindicator and Republican*, July 3, 1903.
Pielak, Lori. *Ghosts of Dallas County*. Quixote Press. 2003.

Chapter 6 - The Van Meter Visitor: A Chronology of Events
"Create A Reign Of Terror" *Emmetsburg Democrat,* Iowa, October 14, 1903.
"Dazzled An Iowa Town" *Newport Hoosier State*, Indiana, November 18, 1903.
"Des Moines' New Monster" *Waterloo Daily Courier*, Iowa October 12, 1903.
Herriute [sp], John Voluntary Observer. "Voluntary Observers Meteorological Record" *U.S. Department of Agriculture, Weather Bureau.* Stuart, Guthrie County Iowa, September 1903.
Herriute [sp], John Voluntary Observer. "Voluntary Observers Meteorological Record" *U.S. Department of Agriculture, Weather Bureau.* Stuart, Guthrie County Iowa, October 1903.
Leonerd [sp], E.J. Voluntary Observer. "Voluntary Observers Meteorological Record" *U.S. Department of Agriculture, Weather Bureau.* Waukee, Dallas County Iowa, September 1903.
Leonerd [sp], E.J. Voluntary Observer. "Voluntary Observers Meteorological Record" *U.S. Department of Agriculture, Weather Bureau.* Waukee, Dallas County Iowa, October 1903.

Minard, R.D. Voluntary Observer. "Voluntary Observers Meteorological Record" *U.S. Department of Agriculture, Weather Bureau*. De Soto, Dallas County Iowa, September 1903.

Minard, R.D. Voluntary Observer. "Voluntary Observers Meteorological Record" *U.S. Department of Agriculture, Weather Bureau*. De Soto, Dallas County Iowa, October 1903.

"Monster Of Awful Form" *Eau Claire Daily Telegram*, Wisconsin, November 19, 1903.

Phillips, Leo Voluntary Observer. "Voluntary Observers Meteorological *Record" U.S. Department of Agriculture, Weather Bureau*. Earlham, Madison County Iowa, September 1903.

Phillips, Leo Voluntary Observer. "Voluntary Observers Meteorological Record" *U.S. Department of Agriculture, Weather Bureau*. Earlham, Madison County Iowa, October 1903.

Sage, J.R. Director. "Monthly Review of the Iowa Weather and Crop Service" *U.S. Department of Agriculture, Weather Bureau*. Central Station, Des Moines Iowa, September 1903.

Sage, J.R. Director. "Monthly Review of the Iowa Weather and Crop Service" *U.S. Department of Agriculture, Weather Bureau*. Central Station, Des Moines Iowa, October 1903.

Special To The Paper. "Town Of Van Meter Wrought Up Over Fishy Story" *Des Moines Daily News*, Iowa, October 4, 1903, page 1.

Special To The World. "This Monster Like A Maniac's Dream" New York World, New York, October 5, 1903.

Special To The Paper. "Van Meter Mystery Is Not Yet Solved" *Des Moines Daily News*, Iowa, October 5, 1903.

"That Winged Monster" *The Evening World*, New York, October 6, 1903.

"Van Meter Hot Under the Collar" *Des Moines Daily Capitol*, Iowa, October 6, 1903.

Voluntary Observer. "Voluntary Observers Meteorological Record" *U.S. Department of Agriculture, Weather Bureau*. Winterset, Madison County Iowa, September 1903.

Chapter 7 - Cryptozoological Derivations: Exploring the Possible Connection to Countless Other Creature Sightings

Bell, Horace. *On The Old West Coast*. 1930.

Coleman, Loren. Cryptozoology A To Z: *The Encycolopedia of Loch Monsters, Sasquatch, Chupacabras, and Other Authentic Mysteries of Nature*. Touchstone, 1999.

Godfrey, Linda S. *The Beast of Bray Road: Trailing Wisconsin's Werewolf*. Madison, WI: Prairie Oak Press, 2003.

Kaku, Michio. *Hyperspace: A Scientific Odyssey Through Parallel Universes, Time Warps, and the 10th Dimension.* Anchor, 1995.

Keel, John A. *The Mothman Prophesies.* New York, NY: Tor, 1991.

-------, *UFOs: Operation Trojan Horse.* New York, NY: Putnam, 1970.

Kelleher, Colm A. and George Knapp. *Hunt for the Skinwalker.* New York, NY: Pocket Books, 2005.

Redfern, Nick. *The Real Men in Black.* Pompton Plains, NJ: New Page Books, 2011.

Talbot, Michael. *The Holographic Universe.* New York, NY: Harper Collins, 1991.

Vallee, Jacques. *Passport to Magonia: From Folklore to Flying Saucers.* Chicago, IL: Henry Regnery Company, 1969.

Chapter 8 - Blatant Hoax or Practical Joker?

Lewis, Chad. *The Most Gruesome Hauntings of the Midwest.* On the Road Publications. 2012.

"Need a Weekly Paper." *Des Moines Daily News*, November 5, 1902.

"Town of Van Meter Badly Wrought Up Over a Fishy Story." *Des Moines Daily News*, October 4, 1903.

"Van Meter Hot Under the Collar." *Des Moines Daily Capitol*, October 6, 1903.

"Van Meter Mystery Not Yet Solved." *Des Moines Daily News*, October 5, 1903.

Chapter 9 - Possible UFO/Alien Connection

Lewis, Chad. *The Wisconsin Road Guide to Mysterious Creatures.* Eau Claire: WI. On The Road Publications. 2011.

Mars, Jim. *Alien Agenda: Investigating the Extraterrestrial Presence Among Us.* New York: NY. Harper Collins. 1997.

"Strange Light Which Bobbed." *Des Moines Daily News*, July 7,1907.

"Was it the Airship." *Waterloo Daily Courier*, April 10, 1897.

"Was it the Airship." *Waterloo Daily Courier*, April 14, 1897

Chapter 10 - Misidentifications: An Examination

Anderson, R. M. 1907. The birds of Iowa. Proceedings of the Davenport Academy of Science 11:125-417.

Beveridge, William I.B. *The Art of Scientific Investigation.* Blackburn Press, 2004.

Cohen, Morris F. *An Introduction To Logic And Scientific Method.* Hughes Press, 2008.

Cornell Laboratory of Ornithology. *Cornell Labe of Ornihology Handbook of Bird Biology*. Princeton University Press, 2004.

Floyd, Ted. *Smithsonian Field Guide to the Birds of North America*. Harper Perennial, 2008.

Kaufman, Kenn. *Lives of North American Birds*. Houghton Mifflin Harcourt, 1996.

Proctor, Noble S. *Manual of Ornithology: Avian Structure and Function*. Yale University Press, 1998.

Chapter 11 - Haunting of the Platt Brick Factory

Brick Factory. www.strangeusa.com. Retrieved December 13, 2012.

Chapter 12 - Mass Hysteria: A Closer Look at the Terror

Maruna, Scott. *The Mad Gasser of Mattoon: Dispelling the Hysteria*. IL. Swamp Gas Book Co. 2003.

Chapter 13 - The Ultraterrestrial Theory: Tricksters, Daimons, and Quantum Consciousness

Anon. *The History of Dallas County, Iowa*. Des Moines, IA: Union Historical Co., 1879.

Devereaux, Paul. *Spirit Roads: An Exploration of Otherworldly Routes*. London, UK: Collins & Brown, 2003.

DuQuette, Lon Milo. *Low Magick: It's All In Your Head ... You Just Have No Idea How Big Your Head Is*. Minneapolis, MN: Llewellyn, 2010.

Hanson, George P. *The Trickster and the Paranormal*. USA: Xlibris, 2001.

Hapur, Patrick. *Daimonic Reality: A Field Guide to the Otherworld*. Enumclaw, WA: Pine Winds Press, 2003.

-------, *The Philosopher's Secret Fire: A History of the Imagination*. Chicago, IL: Ivan R. Dee, 2003.

Holy Bible: Authorized King James Version. Allan-Oxford Longprimer Ref. Ed. Glasgow, UK: R.L.Allan & Son Ltd., 2009.

Keel, John A. *The Mothman Prophesies*. New York, NY: Tor, 1991.

-------, *UFOs: Operation Trojan Horse*. New York, NY: Putnam, 1970.

Kelleher, Colm A. and George Knapp. *Hunt for the Skinwalker*. New York, NY: Pocket Books, 2005.

Michell, John. *The View Over Atlantis*. London, UK: Thames & Hudson Ltd., 1986.

Redfern, Nick. "Lair of the Beasts: Bigfoot: The Problem of Food." www.mania.com/lair-beasts-bigfoot-problem-food_article_137025.html, March 9, 2013.

-------, *The Real Men in Black*. Pompton Plains, NJ: New Page Books, 2011.

Talbot, Michael. *The Holographic Universe*. New York, NY: Harper Collins, 1991.

University of Minnesota. "Radon: Molecular Action and Genetic Effects." http://enhs.umn.edu/hazards/hazardssite/radon/radonmolaction.html, accessed Feb 6, 2013.

Vallee, Jacques. *Confrontations: A Scientist's Search for Alien Contact*. New York, NY: Ballantine Books, 1990.

-------, *Messengers of Deception*. New York, NY: Bantam Books, 1980.

-------, *Passport to Magonia: From Folklore to Flying Saucers*. Chicago, IL: Henry Regnery Company, 1969.

Van Gennep, Arnold. *Rites of Passage*. London, UK: Routledge, 2010.

Watkins, Alfred. *Early British Trackways: Moats, Mounds, Camps and Sites*. London, UK: The Watkins Meter Co., 1921.

Chapter 15 - Early Encounters: Thunderbirds or Thoughtforms?

Armstrong, Hon P.A., *The Piasa, or The Devil Among the Indians*. Morris, IL: E.B. Fletcher, Book and Job Printer, 1887.

Blaine, Martha Royce. *The Ioway Indians*. Oklahoma City, OK: University of Oklahoma Press, 1979.

Godfrey, Linda S. *The Beast of Bray Road: Trailing Wisconsin's Werewolf*. Madison, WI: Prairie Oak Press, 2003.

Reilly III, Kent F. and Garber, James F. (ed.) *Ancient Objects and Sacred Realms: Interpretations of Mississippian Iconography*. Austin, TX: University of Texas Press, 2007.

Owen, Iris S. *Conjuring Up Philip: An Adventure in Psychokinesis*. New York, NY: Harper & Row, 1976.

Senter, Phil. "More 'dinosaur' and 'pterosaur' rock art that isn't." *Palaeontologia Electronica* Vol. 15, Issue 2;22A,14p; http://palaeo-electronica.org/content/2012-issue-2-articles/275-rock-art-dinosaurs, 2012.

Smith, Theresa S. *The Island of the Anishnaabeg: Thunderers and Water Monsters in the Traditional Ojibwe Life-World*. Lincoln, NE: University of Nebraska Press, 2012.

About the Authors

Chad Lewis

For nearly two decades Chad Lewis has traveled the back roads of the world in search of the strange and unusual. From tracking vampires in Transylvania and searching for the elusive monster of Loch Ness to trailing the dangerous Tata Duende through remote villages of Belize and searching for ghosts in Ireland's haunted castles, Chad has scoured the earth in search of the paranormal.

With a Masters Degree in Psychology, Chad has authored 18 books on the supernatural and extensively lectures on his fascinating findings.

The more bizarre the legend, the more likely you'll find Chad there.

Noah Voss

Taking his first EVP in 1986 may have lead Noah Voss to be best known for advancing the use of scientific equipment during investigations into reports of the paranormal. Through GetGhostGear.com, he was first in the world to exclusively offer paranormal investigating equipment for sale in a dedicated online store.

Noah's authored books on local murder mysteries to that of the global UFO enigma in addition to publishing over 4,000 paranormal pages online dating back to 1997. Name the 'ghost' show on TV and he's likely turned them down—helping to keep him more infamous than famous.

Following the back roads since the 1990s has taken Noah through ghostly St. Augustine, Florida, investigating the mysterious Winchester Mansion in California, going for the gone at The Bennington Black Hole in Vermont, haunted highways in Hawaii, looking for Bessie in Lake Erie, trying to get lost in The Bridgewater Triangle of Massachusetts, scanning for flying saucers on the summit of Mount St. Helens, werewolves in Wisconsin, ghosts of Alcatraz in San Francisco Bay, the Historic Bullock Hotel of wild-west Deadwood, the mystery Paulding Lights of Michigan, looking for what went wrong in Salem Massachusetts, prying for Pepie in Lake Pepin on the Mississippi, flying through the Bermuda Triangle, Voodoo in Jamaica, hunting Wendigo-Kan through Canada, UFOs in Mexico, and searching for Sasquatch in British Columbia.

Kevin Lee Nelson

'Unconventional' is the best way to describe Kevin Lee Nelson's theories and research methodology. As an artist and student of Western Esotericism and American folk-magic traditions, Kevin provides a unique perspective enabling him to uncover and decipher symbolic information hidden within various unexplained phenomena. His fascination with sacred geometry and mystical architecture led him to a degree in Drafting & Design Technology.

ABOUT THE AUTHORS

Kevin has investigated hauntings on ABC's *Scariest Places on Earth*, searched for werewolves on Discovery Channel's *Mystery Hunters*, and tracked vampirism in America on Discovery Channel's *Travelers*. He has professionally lectured at conferences across the Midwest for over a decade, and has been a contributing author to a number of books on regional folklore.

Kevin's personal mission is to seek out, record, and preserve our rich heritage of urban legends and modern folklore in order to gain a better understanding of our own personal narratives. This is further illustrated by Kevin's personal library—one of the largest collections of rare books on regional folklore, metaphysics, and parapsychology in the Upper Midwest.

**Real-Life Supernatural Adventures,
Their Hidden Cameras**

No Camera Crew
No 2nd Takes
No Help

~

Simply Dark and Gritty
BackRoadsLore.com

You've read the book,
now see them on location researching,
investigating and adventuring their way
through the Van Meter Iowa area!
Like you've never seen the paranormal before!

**Real-Life Supernatural Adventures,
Their Hidden Cameras**

Visit the site to watch the episodes, get more background
about this legend and many more.

Unearth the next legend alongside them with film
from bizarre locations!
Chat with them live from the back roads!
Tip them off to your local legend!

Continue the adventure at...

TheVanMeterVisitor.com

Discover the latest Van Meter Visitor sightings!
Find all the official Van Meter Visitor event listings!
Hear first where to meet up with the authors and
see them in person next!

Share your experience from Van Meter Iowa and
maybe see itin the 2nd Edition of
The Van Meter Visitor!

TheVanMeterVisitor.com

On The Road Publications
3204 Venus Ave
Eau Claire, WI 54703
www.chadlewisresearch.com